ANTISEMITISM

ALSO BY PHILIP SLAYTON

*Lawyers Gone Bad: Money, Sex and Madness
in Canada's Legal Profession* (2007)

*Mighty Judgment: How the Supreme Court of
Canada Runs Your Life* (2011)

Bay Street: A Novel (2013)

Mayors Gone Bad (2015)

*How to Be Good: The Struggle Between
Law and Ethics* (2017)

The Future of Tennis (2018)

*Nothing Left to Lose: An Impolite Report on the
State of Freedom in Canada* (2020)

ANTISEMITISM

An ancient hatred in the
age of identity politics

PHILIP SLAYTON

SUTHERLAND
HOUSE
TORONTO, 2023

Sutherland House
416 Moore Ave., Suite 205
Toronto, ON M4G 1C9

First edition, March 2023

If you are interested in inviting one of our authors to a live event or
media appearance, please contact sranasinghe@sutherlandhousebooks.com
and visit our website at sutherlandhousebooks.com for more
information about our authors and their schedules.

We acknowledge the support of the Government of Canada.

Manufactured in Canada
Cover designed by Lena Yang
Book composed by Karl Hunt

Library and Archives Canada Cataloguing in Publication
Title: Antisemitism : an ancient hatred in the
age of identity politics / Philip Slayton.
Names: Slayton, Philip, author.
Description: Includes index.
Identifiers: Canadiana (print) 20220453942 | Canadiana (ebook) 20220453950 |
ISBN 9781990823107 (softcover) | ISBN 9781990823091 (EPUB)
Subjects: LCSH: Antisemitism—History. | LCSH: Identity politics.
Classification: LCC DS145 .S62 2023 | DDC 305.892/4009—dc23

ISBN 978-1-990823-10-7
eBook 978-1-990823-09-1

For those who wander the world

CONTENTS

CONTENTS

PREFACE

I had no plans to write a book about antisemitism.[1] But one day in late 2020 a publisher, an old friend of mine from our days together on the PEN Canada board, rang me up and suggested it. "You're the guy," he said.

At first, I wasn't attracted to the idea. I didn't think I was "the guy." Sure, I'd witnessed some antisemitism, and even occasionally experienced mild forms myself, but to me most modern expressions of this ancient prejudice seemed inconsequential and not very interesting. I often thought the way some Jews bemoaned what I regarded as trivial

---

1   There are many different spellings of "antisemitism," e.g., "Anti-Semitism," "Antisemitism". Deborah Lipstadt analyzes the significance of various spellings and adopts "antisemitism," as do I. See her book *Antisemitism Here and Now* (New York: Schocken Books, 2019), pp. 22–25. In 2021 *The New York Times* updated its style guide, replacing "anti-Semitism" with "antisemitism." The Associated Press, the Jewish Telegraphic Agency, and the *Times of Israel* have done the same. It is said that the term "antisemitism" was coined in the late 19th century by Wilhelm Marr, a German. In his 1879 pamphlet *Der Weg zum Siege des Germanenthums über das Judenthum* ("The Way to Victory of Germanism over Judaism") he argued that Jews would use Germany's rights and freedoms to conquer from within. Some have suggested that invention of the neologism "antisemitism" meant that anti-Jewish stereotypes were no longer tied to controversial political and social issues but were, so to speak, free-floating and became a "world view."

incidents of antisemitism was tedious, attention-seeking, and counter-productive. Prominent Jews, Jewish organizations, and much of the media around the world were always complaining about slights and insults that, in my opinion, were best brushed aside or ignored. In their eyes, antisemitism was always "on the increase." What was this, other than a modern extension of the lachrymose conception of Jewish history, the rendition of a "seemingly endless litany of disasters," the portrayal of every calamity in apocalyptic terms, the emphasis on victimhood as "the enduring note of Jewish identity"?[2] And how did you square the idea of the Jew as victim with the muscular Zionism and military kick-ass prowess of Israel, a nuclear-armed regional superpower, and with the great success, in many fields, of Jews who live in the Diaspora? There was something not quite right about the whole antisemitism debate. Or so I thought. And the debate, with its often-confused thinking and silly excesses, didn't help the stability and progress of the international Jewish community and its relations with the rest of the world. So, should I write this book? After my publisher friend called, I asked another friend, a Jewish man with fine literary instincts and credentials, whether he thought this was a good project for me. He knew something of my opinions and said, "Don't do it. You'll upset people, alienate friends, distress relatives."

But, despite my reservations, and the undoubtedly wise advice of my literary friend, I warmed to the possibility. Partly it was because I didn't have much on the go, and needed something to distract me from the unrelenting world health crisis that was then obsessing and debilitating everybody, including me. What better than antisemitism to take your mind off a pandemic? Partly it was because I had a lot of Jewish friends and relatives and felt a connection to that world. Maybe it was time for me to explore this connection and try to understand that world. And, after all, I was Jewish, wasn't I? Or was I? Some would say not: My father was Jewish, but my mother was Roman Catholic.

2   James Carroll, *Constantine's Sword: The Church and the Jews* (New York: Houghton Mifflin, 2001), p. 150.

The modern definition of "Jew" is vague, to say the least. Apparently just about anyone who wants to be a Jew can plausibly claim to be one, including me. On some respectable definitions it doesn't matter if your parents—or even your grandparents—were Jewish, and it certainly doesn't matter that you have no religious beliefs or have not converted to Judaism according to Rabbinical law. You don't even have to be a supporter of the State of Israel. Self-identification is what counts. Am I a Jew? Yes, if I say I am.

Then there was the simple desire to explore a subject I knew little about. The fact I knew little about it—that I had never been immersed in the Jewish world and had not paid much attention to antisemitism— seemed like a good thing. I could approach this difficult topic largely free from initial judgment and prejudice, without an axe to grind. Of course, I had, to some extent, absorbed the standard tropes, without examining them carefully. Throughout history, Jews, a distinct, historic, and unified people, have been subjected to vilification and persecution, and still are; they remain in mortal danger; they have particularly dangerous enemies, notably Arabs and other assorted antisemites; Israel offers safe haven in a land to which Jews have unimpeachable historic, religious, and moral title; the unspeakable tragedy of the Holocaust created a world moral obligation towards the Jewish people; justice is on the side of the Jews. What I didn't know, when I began this book, was how some of these ideas were partly or completely unjustified, or simply not true, and how intellectually and emotionally challenging it would be to analyze and write about them.

Members of the ragtag worldwide collection of self-proclaimed Jews, without a real common language (a key attribute of a nation), for the most part not embracing Judaism as a serious faith, disagree on just about everything, including many policies of the State of Israel, even about whether there should be a State of Israel in the first place. What, if anything, is holding this loose, disputatious, argumentative, agglomeration of people together? Is the international Jewish community a genuine community at all? Or is it, to use the title given by Benedict Anderson to his famous book on nationalism, an imagined community?[3] The prominent French Jewish philosopher Alain Finkielkraut, whose father was a survivor of Auschwitz, has written about what he calls the imaginary Jew: "They're the children and grandchildren of immigrants, handed proud difference as a legacy in trust; they can realize it only through the means they possess: the vaguest reminiscences, a moribund symbolic system and a language that lies in shreds. These are creatures, finally, who have only their imagination to resist the herd. So they don't resist. And to hide their capitulation, they advertise their origin, shout it from the rooftops and become dizzy from the clamor they make. They flaunt their Jewishness, thinking that audacity of gesture can compensate for the irreality it displays."[4]

When Jews are asked what is important to them as Jews, they generally talk, not about religion, but about common ancestry and culture, and commitment to Israel. But, as we shall see, there is little common ancestry and culture, and in recent times commitment to Israel has frayed, notably in the United States and particularly among younger Jews. What is left to bind the community together? There is a mystery here. Is the principal force holding Jews together, ironically, the one thing they fear the most—antisemitism, and its long and anguished history? Jean-Paul Sartre said, "it is the anti-Semite who *makes* the Jew."[5] He wrote: "Jews have neither community of interests nor community of beliefs. They do not have the same fatherland; they have no history. The sole tie that binds them is the hostility and disdain of the societies which surround them."[6] Are Jews as a people only bound together because they are victims of a bizarre, pointless,

---

3   See Benedict Anderson, *Imagined Communities: Reflections on the Origin and Spread of Nationalism* (London: Verso, 2016).

4   Alain Finkielkraut, *The Imagined Jew* (Lincoln: University of Nebraska Press, 1994), p. 96. This book was originally published in 1980 in France with the title *La Juif Imaginaire*.

5   Jean-Paul Sartre, *Anti-Semite and Jew: An Exploration of the Etiology of Hate* (New York: Shocken Books, 1948), p. 69. The original French version of this essay was written in 1944.

6   Sartre, note 5, p. 91.

fraudulent, but deadly, persecution, that has created a tragic history? Do they have nothing else in common?

Most people think they know what antisemitism is, but their conviction doesn't stand up to careful scrutiny. Contemporary definitions are weak, grasping unconvincingly for meaning and content, formulated principally in a political context to serve a political purpose. These definitions blur important distinctions, confuse issues, and inflame passions, sometimes intentionally. They stoke the fires of conflict. They encourage what they purport to police. An international industry ferrets out and publicizes every instance, however trivial, of what is thought to be antisemitism. Antisemitic "incidents" are diligently logged and reported to a variety of organizations. Apparent statistical upticks are noted with apprehension. Every day, warnings about antisemitism are given by respectable institutions and individuals, remedial action is demanded, statements are made, apologies are sought. The process is indiscriminately amplified by social media and by writers described by Yakov Hirsch as "Never Again journalists."[7] Ignorant statements attacking Jews are given a stature they don't deserve. Issues of little consequence are inflated by outrage, encouraged by non-Jewish bystanders including sanctimonious and self-serving government officials pursuing political objectives. Tempers and the temperature rise dangerously. This is not good for anyone. Some expressions of Jew-hatred require a robust response. Others—many—are best ignored. To give equal weight to all expressions of Jew-hatred is to deny serious weight to any.

We need to think differently about antisemitism. We need to discard ideas and attitudes that have been routinely accepted without critical

---

7   Yakov Hirsch, "'Never Again' Journalists Rosenberg, Stephens and Weiss Should Not Speak for the Jews on Colleyville and Antisemitism," *Mondoweiss*, January 27, 2022, https://mondoweiss.net/2022/01/never-again-journalists-rosenberg-stephens-and-weiss-should-not-speak-for-the-jews-on-colleyville-and-antisemitism/ (accessed April 19, 2022). Hirsch argues that "the wrong people are speaking for the Jews on antisemitism," people whose ideas originate in ideology and not scholarship. These people include Bari Weiss and Dara Horne, discussed later in this book. Hirsch writes that "the idea that everyone hates the Jews is highly appealing to many Jews."

appraisal and that have been encouraged by those on both sides of the argument in order to manipulate opinion and politics. We need to understand better both Jewish identity and antisemitism in a new world of assertive and often virulent identity politics. We need to focus on how and by whom antisemitism is expressed, and with what consequences, rather than on pathological motivations and the extreme content of what is said or written or done, which is often incapable of reasoned analysis and rebuttal and not worth serious discussion. The new approach must take into account the source of antisemitism and its nature. Does it come from a thug on the street, an ideologue, a conspiracy theorist, a university professor, a political party, a government official, or a government leader? Is there violence? Distinctions like these make a difference to how we should regard and deal with antisemitism. The new approach must distinguish between what is unacceptable content and action and must be addressed, and how it should be addressed, and what is incoherent, matters little, and should be ignored.

The tale I tell in this book is complicated, tortured, surprising, and often heart-breaking. But there is hope for amity, calm, progress, and peace, if we put history, prejudice, and poor thinking behind us. There is, I believe, a way forward.

CHAPTER 1

ANTISEMITISM AND IDENTITY

WHO AM I? WHERE DO I BELONG?

My father was Jewish, traditionally defined. Both his parents were Jewish, immigrants to England from what was then Russia (now Ukraine) by a circuitous route early in the 20th century. My father certainly regarded himself as Jewish, very much so. He took pride in it. He used a smattering of Yiddish words (*mishigas* was his favourite), told Jewish jokes, and sought out other Jews wherever he lived. Like many Jews of his generation, he was obsessed with the Holocaust. My mother was a non-observant Roman Catholic. Our family didn't go to synagogue, not even on High Holidays. I didn't have a bar mitzvah (my father did). Like Theodor Herzl, the founder of political Zionism, we'd have a Christmas tree every year. My father called it a Hanukkah bush. We thought of ourselves as Jewish, in a vague sort of way, although I was always uncertain about this claim and concerned about my identity, particularly since, on top of everything else, we were immigrants to Canada from England and I retained a slight English accent which confused people and led to my being taunted in the school yard when

I was a child. I was an immigrant, half Jewish (let's say), a kid with an English accent—I felt like an outsider then, someone who didn't quite fit in, even in Canada. I still feel that way to some degree, although I've lived in Canada for almost seventy years. For an immigrant, the outsider feeling doesn't go away easily, if ever. As for the Jewish part, as Alain Finkielkraut writes, "The game of 'Who am I?' will be a short one, for the Jewish content of our lives isn't enough to rub two sticks together."[8]

The ambiguous identity I grappled with as a child, with its accompanying personal uncertainty and nervousness, followed me through my professional life as a lawyer. Sometimes it led to unpleasant dilemmas. Generally, colleagues and clients didn't think of me as Jewish. I didn't look particularly Jewish, my name wasn't obviously a Jewish name, and there was that slight English accent which threw people off. Occasionally, at a meeting I was attending, or in casual conversation, someone would make an antisemitic remark. I never said or did anything when this happened. I let it pass. I knew that it wouldn't help my career to criticize an important client or colleague, or leave a meeting on a point of principle. It wouldn't advance my personal interests if I caused an incident that embarrassed people and made them feel uncomfortable. I'm ashamed of how I behaved on those occasions.

Am I Jewish or not? According to well-accepted contemporary definitions I discuss below, I'm "partly Jewish" or part of the "net" Jewish population. But according to these definitions, pretty much anyone who wants to be Jewish is Jewish. It's just a matter of self-identification. How much does that help someone who is uncertain about his identity? What you want is community endorsement. Your identity is mostly decided not, by you, but by what other people think about you. The self-identification approach certainly wouldn't have worked when I was growing up on the periphery of Winnipeg's Jewish

8   Finkielkraut, note 4, p. 95.

community. Winnipeg Jews knew who belonged and who didn't, and self-identification didn't enter into it.

WHO IS A JEW?

Who is a Jew? It's a big tent. Rabbinical law holds that a Jew is someone with a Jewish mother or who has properly converted to the Jewish religion. Accepted modern scholarship and analysis are far more accommodating. Sergio DellaPergola, a leading expert on Jewish statistics and demographics, identifies four Jewish groups, based largely on self-identification.[9] The DellaPergola groups cover enormous ground. There is the "core" Jewish population, people who consider Judaism their exclusive identity. There are those who say they are "partly Jewish" because they claim other identities as well. There is the "enlarged" Jewish population which includes those who claim a Jewish background although they do not have a Jewish parent. There is the Law of Return population, which includes those who have one Jewish grandparent.[10] Within these four broad groups, there is room for

9   Sergio DellaPergola, "World Jewish Population, 2018," in Arnold Dashefsky and Ira M. Sheskin (editors), *The American Jewish Year Book, 2018* (Dordrecht: Springer), pp. 361–452 https://www.jewishdatabank.org/content/upload/bjdb/2018-World_Jewish_Population_(AJYB,_DellaPergola)_DB_Final.pdf (accessed December 11, 2020), pp. 10–11. See also Sergio DellaPergola and L. Daniel Staetsky, *Jews in Europe at the Turn of the Millennium*, Institute for Jewish Policy Research, European Jewish Demography Unit, October 2020, p. 12 https://www.jpr.org.uk/documents/JPR_2020.Jews_in_Europe_at_the_turn_of_the_Millennium.pdf (accessed March 26, 2021).

10 The 1950 Israeli Law of Return provides that Jews who immigrate to Israel have an immediate right to citizenship. A 1970 amendment to the Law provides "The rights of a Jew under this Law . . . are also vested in a child and a grandchild of a Jew, the spouse of a Jew, the spouse of a child of a Jew and the spouse of a grandchild of a Jew . . ." In February 2021 the Israeli Supreme Court granted the right to automatic citizenship to foreigners who convert within the State of Israel to Conservative or Reform Judaism. Orthodox Jews in Israel had long resisted this as well as the role of the Supreme Court in deciding such matters. See Patrick Kingsley, "Israeli Court Says Converts to Non-Orthodox Judaism Can Claim Citizenship," *The New York*

many national backgrounds, substantial religious differences, different languages, a wide range of cultural practices, and radically different political opinions. As David Graham's 2019 study of South African Jews comments, "Jewish identity is a multi-dimensional concept and no single measure can describe it satisfactorily."[11]

The 2013 Pew Research Center study of American Jews took an approach similar to DellaPergola's.[12] It defined the "net" Jewish population as consisting of two groups, Jews who say their religion is Jewish and who do not profess any other religion, and Jews who describe themselves as atheist, agnostic, or nothing in particular, but who have a Jewish parent or were raised Jewish and who still consider themselves Jewish in some way (sometimes referred to as "Jews of No Religion" or JNR). The Pew survey also included non-Jewish people of Jewish background (people who have a Jewish parent or were raised Jewish but who, today, either have another religion or say they do not consider themselves Jewish) and non-Jewish people who consider themselves Jewish for some ill-defined reason.

Times, March 1, 2021 https://www.nytimes.com/2021/03/01/world/middleeast/israel-jewish-converts-citizenship.html (accessed March 2, 2021). A further ruling of the Israeli Supreme Court in August 2021 clarified "that a non-Jewish widow or widower whose deceased spouse was a child or grandchild of a Jew has the right to immigrate to Israel and receive all the privileges and benefits of a Jewish new immigrant . . ." See Joshua Pex, "Interpretation of the Law of Return," *Israel Today* October 18, 2021 https://www.israeltoday.co.il/read/israel-supreme-court-expands-interpretation-of-the-law-of-return/ (accessed October 18, 2021).

11 See David Graham, *The Jews of South Africa in 2019* (London/Cape Town: Institute for Jewish Policy Research and Kaplan Centre for Jewish Studies, 2020), p. 29. http://www.kaplancentre.uct.ac.za/sites/default/files/image_tool/images/151/2020/The_Jews_of_South_Africa_in_2019March2020.pdf (accessed January 8, 2021).

12 "Who Is a Jew?" https://www.pewforum.org/2013/10/01/sidebar-who-is-a-jew/ (accessed January 21, 2021).

WHAT IS ANTISEMITISM?

Everyone needs someone to hate. William Hazlitt, the 19[13]-century English essayist, wrote, "hatred alone is immortal."[13] The Quran, the sacred scripture of Islam, in an early expression of identity politics, says, "We make for every prophet an adversary."[14] Hatred has driven much of the world's history. Jews are a time-honoured and preferred object of hatred. There are, of course, other objects of hatred, today and throughout history—hatred of others, anybody, is a pervasive human phenomenon. The Israeli politician Yair Lapid controversially suggested in a 2021 speech in Jerusalem that antisemitism was not unique "but one bigotry among many in the rich and variegated mosaic of human hatred." But Benjamin Netanyahu, another one-time Israeli prime minister, responded, "While antisemitism, hatred of Jews, is part of the general human phenomenon of hatred of others, it's different from it in intensity, in its durability over millennia, and in the murderous ideology nurtured for generations to prepare the way for the extermination of the Jews."[15]

Hatred of Jews was initially religious and then became racial. This change meant that religious conversion, often forced and always suspect,[16] no longer offered safety and assimilation into nationalist

13 William Hazlitt, *On the Pleasure of Hating* (Monee, IL: Pantianos Classics, 2021), p. 122.
14 See David Nirenberg, *Anti-Judaism: The Western Tradition* (New York: W.W. Norton, 2013), chapter 4.
15 Quoted by Haviv Rettig Gur, "A Hatred That Dwells Alone? Antisemitism Debate Cuts to Heart of Zionist Vision," *The Times of Israel*, July 26, 2021 https://www.timesofisrael.com/a-hatred-that-dwells-alone-antisemitism-debate-cuts-to-heart-of-zionist-vision/ (accessed August 2, 2021).
  And see Lapid's Facebook post, July 15, 2021, for the text of his speech https://www.facebook.com/107836625941364/posts/4337787169612934/?d=n (accessed August 2, 2021).
16 Conversion of Jews to Christianity was particularly popular in Spain in the years leading up to the Spanish Inquisition and expulsion of the Jews in 1492. On "conversos," see Erna Paris, *The End of Days* (Amherst: Prometheus Books, 1995), particularly chapter 7.

societies. Racial origin—purity of blood—was what counted. Jews were eternally contaminated. That was the whole point. This was the approach of Nazi Germany. The Nuremberg Laws of September 1935, in defining a Jew, relied on bloodlines and nothing else (a Jew was someone with at least one Jewish grandparent). The racial underpinning of antisemitism was discredited by the history of the Third Reich, and was replaced by fluid political and ideological identification of Jews. This is the third phase of antisemitism, which prevails today.[17] The implications of the third phase are important. Jews are no longer identified by religion or race, but by other complex and controversial criteria, which can shift for political and other reasons. So, for example, as Finkielkraut points out, Jews become "Zionists" and antisemitism then becomes anti-Zionism. "In our era," he writes, "we persecute ideologies, not whole peoples: there are no more sub-human species, just the henchmen of imperialism, fascists hiding behind the shield of the blue star of David . . ."[18] He writes, "For radical anti-Zionists, the Jew does not exist."[19] Here is a good place to make the point that although the modern definition of Jew, as we have seen, depends on self-identification, others looking from the outside may not agree with this approach and may use different criteria.

Antisemitism may be more opportunistic than ideological; this was particularly true in the 19th century. If you dislike a social or political development but don't want to confront it head on (because to do so would be unbecoming or unpolitic), then rather than damning the unwanted development explicitly, you can associate it with Jews and attack them instead. Phyllis Goldstein, in her sweeping history of antisemitism, calls it "a convenient hatred."[20] Harvard historian Ruth Wisse has written, "If

---

17 See Bernard Lewis, "The New Antisemitism," *The American Scholar*, December 1, 2005 https://theamericanscholar.org/the-new-anti-semitism/ (accessed August 20, 2021).

18 Finkielkraut, note 4, p. 148.

19 Finkielkraut, note 4, p. 164.

20 Phyllis Goldstein, *A Convenient Hatred: The History of Antisemitism* (Brookline: Facing History and Ourselves, 2012).

you're a politician or leader, you reach for an implement that's handy. In a sense, the Jews were handy."[21] Wisse considers antisemitism to be primarily an ideology serving a political purpose and having political utility. She writes, "anti-Semitism became a stand-in for opposition to liberalizing reforms, and a substitute for real evidence of harms done by liberalism to the societies in which it was advancing."[22]

In a 1962 letter to his nephew, written just before the one hundredth anniversary of the American emancipation of slaves, James Baldwin wrote: "This innocent country set you down in a ghetto in which, in fact, it intended that you should perish . . . You were born where you were born and faced the future that you faced because you were black and *for no other reason*."[23] Jews, like blacks, are attacked because they are Jewish—and *for no other reason*. Barack Obama echoed the language of James Baldwin when he said in a September 21, 2011, speech to the United Nations General Assembly, "The Jewish people carry the burden of centuries of exile and persecution, and fresh memories of knowing that six million people were killed simply because of who they are."[24] Bernard Lewis (and others) has observed the parallels between persecution of the Jews and the enslavement and maltreatment of black people. He has described them as "the two most appalling and widespread manifestations of racism in the nineteenth and twentieth centuries."[25] But Lewis noted one important difference. The antisemite wants to destroy the Jew. The black hater seeks, not to destroy the black person, but to dominate, humiliate, and use him. All this, of course, puts to one side the thorny question of exactly who is a Jew for the purposes of persecution.

21 See Haviv Rettig Gur, note 15.
22 Ruth R. Wisse, "The Functions of Anti-Semitism," *National Affairs* Fall 2017 https:// www.nationalaffairs.com/publications/detail/the-functions-of-anti-semitism (accessed August 2, 2021).
23 James Baldwin, *The Fire Next Time* (New York: Vintage International, 1993), p. 7.
24 "Full Transcript of Obama's Speech at UN General Assembly," *Haaretz*, September 21, 2011 https://www.haaretz.com/1.5180811 (accessed July 25, 2021).
25 Bernard Lewis, *Semites and Anti-Semites* (London: Phoenix, 1997), p. 22.

If antisemitism has political utility for those who oppose liberalizing reforms, it also perversely has political and cultural utility for the Jews themselves. In the Preface to this book I quoted Jean-Paul Sartre: "Jews have neither community of interests nor community of beliefs. They do not have the same fatherland; they have no history. The sole tie that binds them is the hostility and disdain of the societies which surround them."[26] Anticipating Sartre, Stefan Zweig, an Austrian Jew, wrote in 1942, "the Jews of the twentieth century were not a community any more, nor had they been for a long time. They had no faith in common with each other, they felt their Jewish identity was a burden rather than a source of pride . . . They were increasingly impatient to integrate with the lives of the people around them and become part of their communities, dispersing into society in general . . . As a result they no longer understood each other, having become part of those other nations—they were more French, German, British and Russian that they were Jews." But then, wrote Zweig, Nazi Germany and the Holocaust, in the most horrible of ways, brought them together: "Only now were Jews forced, for the first time in centuries, to be a single community again."[27] Now, things are different. Peter Beinart writes, "Today . . . the decline of anti-Semitism has made it easy to stop being Jewish."[28] Shlomo Sand writes that secular Jewish identity—the identity of Jews who are not religious—is based only on a dead past: "Knowing that there is no specific mode of everyday life that could bind together secular individuals of Jewish origin across the world, it is impossible to

---

26 Jean-Paul Sartre, note 5, p. 91. Others have made similar analyses, e.g., the French Islamic scholar Maxime Rodinson: "Jewish identity in twentieth century Europe was but a residual phenomenon." (Quoted by Susie Linfield, *The Lion's Den: Zionism and the Left from Hannah Arendt to Noam Chomsky* (New Haven: Yale University Press, 2019), p. 123.) Rodinson was Jewish and his parents died in Auschwitz. He wrote a brilliant biography of the Prophet Mohammed: *Muhammad* (New York: New York Review Books, 2021), originally published in 1961 in French as *Mahomet*.

27 Stefan Zweig, *The World of Yesterday* (Lincoln: University of Nebraska Press, 2013), pp. 453–4.

28 Peter Beinart, *The Crisis of Zionism* (New York: Picador, 2012), p. 183.

assert the existence either of a living, non-religious Jewish culture or of a possible common future, apart from the vestiges handed down from a declining religious tradition."[29]

Sartre asks, who is the anti-Semite? "He considers himself an average man, modestly average, basically mediocre . . . This man fears every kind of solitariness . . . [H]e is the man of the crowd . . . He has made himself an anti-Semite because that is something one cannot be alone . . . [T]here is a passionate pride among the mediocre, and anti-Semitism is an attempt to give value to mediocrity as such, to create an elite of the ordinary."[30] Antisemitism is hatred expressed by a mediocre person seeking to join other mediocre people to order together their drab and unsatisfying world.[31]

Mediocre people often band together and acquire political power (there are many contemporary examples of this phenomenon). Democracy and mass movements, the organization and mobilization of the mediocre, can intensify antisemitism. Götz Aly notes, "The social rise of the European masses bolstered rather than lessened anti-Jewish resentment." In pre-World War I Italy, for example, limited voting rights "basically ruled out the development of organized anti-Semitism."[32] This changed. Aly writes, "The hope of easily enriching oneself and quickly rising up the social ladder was a general motivation for twentieth-century ethnic violence and a significant contributor to the discrimination, persecution, and murder of European Jews."[33] And then, at the end of his book reviewing in great detail European antisemitism in the period 1880–1945, Aly reaches a startling conclusion: "Well-intentioned educational policies and state-supported desires to lift the masses socially—both of which can be counted

29 Shlomo Sand, *How I Stopped Being a Jew* (London: Verso, 2014), p. 22.
30 Sartre, note 5, pp. 22–23.
31 How this works is vividly described, in shocking detail, in Daniel Jonah Goldhagen, *Hitler's Willing Executioners: Ordinary Germans and the Holocaust* (New York: Alfred A. Knopf, 1996).
32 Götz Aly, *Europe Against the Jews 1880–1945* (New York: Picador, 2017), pp. 314–5.
33 Aly, note 32, p. 317.

among twentieth-century Europe's great triumphs—served to increase hatred. The same is also true of the best political ideas and those most deserving of continuation: democracy, liberty, popular participation, self-determination, and social equality."[34]

Sartre's mediocre men are often conspiracy theorists. The 2021 Jerusalem Declaration on Antisemitism (JDA) (discussed below) said: "What is particular in classic antisemitism is the idea that Jews are linked to the forces of evil. This stands at the core of many anti-Jewish fantasies, such as the idea of a Jewish conspiracy in which 'the Jews' possess hidden power that they use to promote their own collective agenda at the expense of other people. This linkage between Jews and evil continues in the present: in the fantasy that 'the Jews' control governments with a 'hidden hand,' that they own the banks, control the media, act as 'a state within a state,' and are responsible for spreading disease (such as Covid-19)."[35] Sartre explained how conspiracy theory works as false reasoning: "How can one choose to reason falsely? It is because of a longing for impenetrability. The rational man groans as he gropes for the truth; he knows that his reasoning is no more than tentative, that other considerations may supervene to cast doubt on it. He never sees very clearly where he is going; he is 'open'; he may even appear to be hesitant. But there are people who are attracted by the durability of a stone . . . They do not want any acquired opinions; they want them to be innate. Since they are afraid of reasoning, they wish to lead the kind of life wherein reasoning and research play only a subordinate role, wherein one seeks only what he has already found, wherein one becomes only what he already was."[36] Karen Douglas, an American psychologist and writer on conspiracy theories, has suggested that people are attracted to such theories when important psychological needs are not being met. She identifies three such needs: the need for knowledge and certainty; the need to feel safe and

34 Aly, note 32, p. 335.
35 2021 Jerusalem Declaration on Antisemitism, https://jerusalemdeclaration.org/
36 Sartre, note 5, pp. 18–19.

secure when powerless and scared; and the need to feel unique.[37] The conspiracy theorist seeks a comforting narrative that makes him feel better. Dara Horne argues that antisemitism is "at heart a conspiracy theory, and one appeal of conspiracy theories is that they absolve their believers of accountability, replacing the difficult obligation to build relationships with the easy urge to destroy."[38]

In May 2016, the International Holocaust Remembrance Alliance (IHRA), an intergovernmental organization founded in 1998, adopted a "working definition" of antisemitism: "Antisemitism is a certain perception of Jews, which may be expressed as hatred toward Jews. Rhetorical and physical manifestations of antisemitism are directed toward Jewish or non-Jewish individuals and/or their property, toward Jewish community institutions and religious facilities."[39] Several "examples" of antisemitism are given by the IHRA to explain and illustrate this general and vague definition, for instance, accusing the Jews as a people, or Israel as a state, of inventing or exaggerating the Holocaust; accusing Jewish citizens of being more loyal to Israel, or to the alleged priorities of Jews worldwide, than to the interests of their own nations; denying the Jewish people their right to self-determination, for example, by claiming that the existence of a State of Israel is a racist endeavor; applying double standards by requiring of Israel a behaviour not expected or demanded of any other democratic nation; and holding Jews collectively responsible for actions of the State of Israel. Notwithstanding its obvious flaws, the IHRA definition has proved highly influential, ceremonially adopted (an easy thing to do, since adopting it has no particular consequences) by many, including President Joe Biden, the city of Paris, the states of Kentucky

37 Referred to by Thomas Edsall, "The QAnon Delusion Has Not Loosened Its Grip," *The New York Times,* February 3, 2021 https://www.nytimes.com/2021/02/03/opinion/qanon-conspiracy-theories.html (accessed February 15, 2021).

38 Dara Horne, *People Love Dead Jews: Reports from a Haunted Present* (New York: W.W. Norton, 2021), p. 187.

39 For the full text of the IHRA working definition and a list of the many who have adopted it, see International Holocaust Remembrance Alliance, https://www.holocaustremembrance.com/resources/working-definitions-charters/working-definition-antisemitism (accessed April 21, 2021).

and Texas, the Village of Great Neck on Long Island, the Secretary-General of the United Nations, the European Union, the English Football Association, the Italian premier soccer league, the Israeli Knesset (parliament), Lufthansa, Oxford and Cambridge universities, and many national governments including those of Israel, Canada, the United Kingdom, and Germany.

To some people, enthusiastic endorsement and adoption of the IHRA definition has become a test of bona fides in the "fight" against antisemitism. But to others, the definition is obviously inadequate and even dangerous. Some have said that it is too vague, or stifles free speech—for example, by obstructing campaigning for the rights of Palestinians—or unreasonably conflates criticism of Israel with antisemitism.[40] A group of distinguished U.K. lawyers called the definition "incoherent" and possessing no domestic or international legal authority.[41] Others have called it "a mess."[42] In Canada, 150 Jewish academics, in a March 2021 statement on the IHRA definition, "highlighted the level of 'lobbying' on campuses to have it adopted and the 'intimidation' and silencing of free speech at those universities that have already adopted the draft." Said the group: "We add our

40 See Arno Rosenfeld, "Thirty-nine Words About Antisemitism Are Splitting the Jewish Community," *Forward*, January 26, 2021 https://forward.com/news/462859/ihra-definition-conference-of-presidents-opposition-antisemitism/ (accessed January 27, 2021). Also, Larry Haiven, "How the IHRA Definition of Antisemitism Is Used to Muzzle Criticism of Israel—the Winnipeg Example," *Mondoweiss*, July 26, 2021 https://mondoweiss.net/2021/07/how-the-ihra-definition-of-antisemitism-is-used-to-muzzle-criticism-of-israel-the-winnipeg-example/ (accessed July 30, 2021).

41 "Antisemitism Definition Is Undermining Free Speech," *The Guardian*, January 7, 2021 https://www.theguardian.com/news/2021/jan/07/antisemitism-definition-is-undermining-free-speech (accessed July 30, 2021). See also, Harriet Sherwood, "Williamson Wrong to Force Universities to Abide by Antisemitism Definition, Say Lawyers," *The Guardian*, January 7, 2021 https://www.theguardian.com/politics/2021/jan/07/williamson-wrong-to-force-universities-to-abide-by-antisemitism-definition-say-lawyers (accessed July 30, 2021).

42 Gary Sinyor, "IHRA Line by Line: A Mess- and an Alternative," *The Times of Israel*, January 28, 2021 https://blogs.timesofisrael.com/ihra-line-by-line-a-mess-and-an-alternative/ (accessed January 29, 2021).

voices to a growing international movement of Jewish scholars to insist that university policies to combat anti-Semitism are not used to stifle legitimate criticisms of the Israeli state, or the right to stand in solidarity with the Palestinian people . . ."[43] In November 2021, the Canadian Association of University Teachers, with more than 70,000 members, rejected the IHRA definition. The CAUT said that it "supports the academic freedom of its members and recognises the need to safeguard the rights of scholars to critique all states, including the State of Israel, without fear of outside political influence, cuts to funding, censorship, harassment, threats, and intimidation."[44]

In my view, the IHRA definition is vague, unhelpful, imprecise, poorly crafted, absurdly broad, dangerous to free speech, and a stimulus to conflict. It falls into the trap of focussing on content (in the most unconvincing of ways) rather than on the way and by whom content is expressed.

In March 2021, responding to the IHRA definition, more than 200 Jewish scholars released the Jerusalem Declaration on Antisemitism offering a different core definition of antisemitism.[45] The Jerusalem Declaration defines antisemitism as "discrimination, prejudice, hostility or violence against Jews as Jews (or Jewish institutions as Jewish)." It specifically excludes from the definition efforts to boycott Israel. Says the Declaration: "Boycott, divestment, and sanctions are commonplace, non-violent forms of political protest against states. In the Israeli case, they are not, in and of themselves, antisemitic." It says, "Because the IHRA Definition is unclear in key respects and widely

---

43 "Jewish Faculty Members in Canada Oppose Adoption of IHRA Antisemitism Definition," *The Palestine Chronicle*, March 29, 2021 https://www.palestinechronicle. com/jewish-faculty-members-in-canada-oppose-adoption-of-ihra-antisemitism-definition/ (accessed March 30, 2021).

44 "Canada: Academics Vote to Reject IHRA Definition of Anti-Semitism," *Middle East Monitor*, December 2, 2021 https://www.middleeastmonitor.com/20211202-canada-academics-vote-to-reject-ihra-definition-of-anti-semitism/ (accessed December 8, 2021).

45 For the full text of the Jerusalem Declaration, accompanying commentary and guidelines, and a list of its signatories, see https://jerusalemdeclaration.org/

open to different interpretations, it has caused confusion and generated controversy, hence weakening the fight against antisemitism." The Jerusalem Declaration aims "to protect a space for an open debate about the vexed question of the future of Israel/Palestine." It is not antisemitic, said the Declaration, to support "the Palestinian demand for justice and the full grant of their political, national, civil and human rights," or to make evidence-based criticism of Israel as a state. Similar statements were made at about the same time by the Nexus Task Force, a liberal group of Jewish scholars, in the so-called "Nexus Document."[46]

The American writer and feminist Letty Cottin Pogrebin points out that all three approaches to defining antisemitism—those of the IHRA, JDA, and the Nexus Document—give Israel an outsized role, this although "most antisemitic hate speech, vandalism or violence is expressed as personal or group animus toward Jews as Jews, without reference to the Jewish state." She argues that those who pursue an official definition "seem to be motivated, in large part, by the desire to conflate Israel with Jews and condemnation of Israeli policy with Jew-hating . . . Thus has antisemitism, the one issue that used to unite Jews, become a wedge to divide us, and Israel a bludgeon."[47]

THE HOLOCAUST

The incomprehensible tragedy of the Holocaust, one of the greatest crimes of history, informs and explains almost everything to do with modern Jewry. It is almost unbearable to read about and reflect on this event. You carry the horror of it always once it has entered your mind.

---

46 See Ron Kampeas, "Over 200 Scholars Create New Antisemitism Definition Excluding BDS," *The Jerusalem Post*, March 26, 2021 https://www.jpost.com/diaspora/over-200-scholars-create-new-antisemitism-definition-excluding-bds-663277 (accessed March 27, 2021).
47 Letty Cottin Pogrebin, "We Know It When We See It," *Moment*, September/October 2021 https://momentmag.com/opinion-we-know-it-when-we-see-it/ (accessed September 30, 2021).

Knowledge of the Holocaust easily invests deadly significance in what would otherwise be considered the most trivial of antisemitic slights. It can throw a blanket of suspicion and fear over inconsequential and innocent interactions between Jews and non-Jews. For some, understandably, it makes it presumptuous, perhaps impossible, to pass any judgment or make any criticism of Jewish sensitivity to any kind of antagonism, however irrational and exaggerated that sensitivity might otherwise seem. The Holocaust is always there, in history and imagination, a window through which everything is seen and everything is understood, in the blackest of terms. David Baddiel writes about, "how scared, at base, Jews are. Jews, particularly those of my generation, were brought up under the shadow of the Holocaust. My mother was born in Nazi Germany. I only exist by the skin of my teeth . . . Jews have this reference point, a terrible one, but intellectually an inescapable one. We have the advantage . . . of having an objective corollary of what happens when anti-Semitism is allowed to run unchecked."[48] James Carroll asks, "Does the very act of thinking about the Holocaust . . . diminish its horror by refusing to treat it as unthinkable?"[49] The Holocaust is unthinkable. It shatters all categories of meaning.

IDENTITY POLITICS AND THE
TWILIGHT OF CITIZENSHIP

The American political scientist Frances Fukuyama writes that personal identity comes from distinguishing between one's inner self and an outer world that may not adequately recognize your inner worth. In modern times, Fukuyama argues, the view has taken hold "that the authentic inner self is intrinsically valuable, and the outer society systematically wrong and unfair in its valuation of the former. It is not

---

48 David Baddiel, *Jews Don't Count: How Identity Politics Failed One Particular Identity* (London: TLS Books, 2021), pp. 108–9.
49 James Carroll, note 2, p. 6.

the inner self that has to be made to conform to society's rules, but society itself that needs to change."[50] The moral idea of identity, says Fukuyama, "focuses our natural demand for recognition of our dignity and gives us a language for expressing the resentments that arise when such recognition is not forthcoming."[51]

The modern world is replete with multiplying identity groups, each one constantly shrinking in size and splintering as its members, pursuing their "authentic inner self" in the face of an allegedly unfair outer society, refine their personal identities with greater and greater precision and leave to form an even smaller and even more distinctive group. These groups and their members typically claim to be oppressed, marginalized, and victimized. They demand many things: dignity, attention, respect, visibility, status, sympathy, recognition of difference, the exclusive right to express their culture, an end to colonialism, freedom from criticism, redress for historical grievances and humiliation, and political and economic power (political and economic power is less important to most of these groups than one might expect). Often full of resentment, burning with a sense of victimization, these groups compete with each other, for tired humankind does not have enough respect, attention, and sympathy for everyone. They define themselves, not only by what they are, but by what they're not ("the assertion of an identity always proceeds through contrast or opposition"[52]). They can be combative, suspicious, ready to attack, and contemptuous of other groups. Any argument from an outsider that questions their identity, however rational and reasonable, is regarded as illegitimate. Members of identity groups argue that only someone who has lived a life with their identity ("lived experience"[53]) can understand them

---

50 Francis Fukuyama, *Identity: The Demand for Dignity and the Politics of Resentment* (New York: Picador, 2018), pp. 9–10.
51 Fukuyama, note 50, p. 163.
52 Kwame Anthony Appiah, *The Lies That Bind: Rethinking Identity* (New York: Liveright, 2018), p. 202.
53 The South African philosopher David Benatar has observed: "The kernel of truth is that experiencing something oneself *can* sometimes give one an insight that

("the tribal instinct is not just an instinct to belong. It is also an instinct to exclude."[54]). They are aggressively skeptical of the credentials of those who seek to join their ranks. Their demands are non-negotiable. Sometimes the result is a successful, just, moral, and long-overdue political expression of a long-repressed and oppressed social identity, producing welcome change in public policy and attitudes (gay rights, for example); the world becomes a better place. Sometimes the battle descends into bitterness, confusion, and division, and the world gets worse.

Modern identity politics is a vague echo of 19th-century European nationalism. Götz Aly writes, "In the nineteenth century, nationalism blossomed as a romantic springtime of various peoples . . . European nationalists dedicated themselves to the social emancipation of their own native groups."[55] Until political Zionism was born, there was no part for Jews in this emancipation process. Indeed, nationalism in the societies where Jews lived was dangerous for them. In 19th- and 20th-century European history "General battle cries like *'la France pour les français'* or *'Polska dla Polaków'* were all too often specifically directed against Jews."[56] Aly argues that nationalism quickly leads to nationalization, often "a euphemism for expropriating what was owned by people branded as foreigners." Nationalists routinely branded Jews as foreigners as a prelude to seizing their property. Old-fashioned nationalism, of course, is mostly about the attempts of well-defined

is lacking in others who know of something only through the reports of those experiencing them. The problem is that experiences can also be mistaken. There is a conceptual difference between perception and reality. Some perceptions are mistaken." See David Benatar, *The Fall of the University of Cape Town* (Politicsweb Publishing, 2021), p. 11. The American philosopher Tom Nagel would likely support the importance of lived experience. In his famous 1974 paper "What Is It Like to Be a Bat?" Nagel concluded that only a bat knew what it was like to be a bat. See http://www.philosopher.eu/others-writings/nagel-what-is-it-like-to-be-a-bat/ (accessed August 18, 2022).

54 Amy Chua, *Political Tribes: Group Instinct and the Fate of Nations* (New York: Penguin, 2019), p. 1.

55 Aly, note 32, p. 309.

56 Aly, note 32, p. 310.

groups to seize political power (and the property of others) and become self-governing in a defined territory, always to the detriment of those outside the group. As I have mentioned, 21st-century identity groups, for the time being at least (and with some exceptions—e.g., Indigenous peoples), are not much interested in political power and self-government. Nor are they interested in seizing land or other property (again with some exceptions). Their springtime is a different springtime from that of old-fashioned nationalists, but it is still romantic.

Identity can be a function of just about any characteristic—religion, ethnicity, race, gender, sexual orientation, age, family background, social and economic class, disability, neurological status, education, food history and preferences, intelligence, cultural attainment (can you play the violin or kalimba, or speak French or Inuktitut?), language, political belief (particularly attitudes towards immigration and refugees), geography, and so on. An individual or group can adopt more than one label, creating a hyper-specific identity. This is known as intersectionality, and is said to be a way of escaping the tyranny of "a single axis." Intersectionality acknowledges the possibility of overlapping forms of discrimination, an overlapping that compounds suffering. Identity politics (intersectionality included) can embrace Catalan, Quebec or Scottish separatists, Northern Ireland Catholics, LGBTQ women of colour, white male supremacists, black feminists, Muslim Americans, Brexiteers, anti-vaxxers, transgender Latinos, Palestinians, Islamists, Jews of Colour (JoC),[57] you name it. Paradoxically, individual identity can be easily subsumed or repressed by a group identity based on shared characteristics.[58]

---

57 See Jews of Color Initiative, *Beyond the Count: Perspectives and Lived Experiences of Jews of Color* (2021) https://jewsofcolorinitiative.org/wp-content/uploads/2021/08/BEYONDTHECOUNT.FINAL_.8.12.21.pdf?utm_source=JoCI+website&utm_medium=PDF&utm_campaign=Beyond+the+Count+report (accessed August 25, 2021).

58 For the extreme difficulty in establishing a clear identity, and on the tendency of individuals in a group to exaggerate their sameness, see Appiah, note 52. Appiah rejects what he calls "essentialism," an essence of identity that survives across time and space.

Identity politics, buttressed in some cases by critical race theory as its handmaiden, rejects universalism in favour of particularism, liberalism in favour of tribalism. It emphasizes individual cultural issues and ignores the complex nature of major problems, such as climate change, which cut across particular identities. It turns its back upon traditional ideals that transcend group divides—the idea, for example, that skin colour doesn't matter, an idea sometimes said, these days, to be a stalking horse for white privilege or supremacy. It repudiates universalist philosophical movements, including the concept of universal human rights. It rejects the rhetoric of Martin Luther King Jr.: "I have a dream that my four little children will one day live in a nation where they will not be judged by the color of their skin, but by the content of their character."[59] It rejects the rhetoric of Barack Obama: "There's not a Black America and a White America and Latino America and Asian America—there's the United States of America."[60] It rejects the ideal, embraced by post-revolutionary France and other countries and societies, that all citizens have equal rights as individuals, not groups. It denies justice as fairness, if you believe— as many still do—in the original position and veil of ignorance tests of the great 20th-century political and legal philosopher John Rawls.[61] "Rawls holds that the fact that a citizen is of a certain race, class, and

---

59 From the famous speech delivered on August 28, 1963, from the steps of the Lincoln Memorial in Washington D.C. This remark is sometimes quoted out-of-context by right-wing American politicians as part of an attack on critical race theory. See, e.g., Jennifer Schuessler, "Ted Cruz Invokes Dr. King, and Scholars See a Familiar Distortion," *The New York Times*, March 23, 2022 https://www. nytimes.com/2022/03/23/arts/ted-cruz-mlk-critical-race-theory-supreme-court. html?referringSource=articleShare (accessed April 20, 2022).

60 See "Barack Obama's Remarks to the Democratic National Convention," *The New York Times*, July 27, 2004 https://www.nytimes.com/2004/07/27/politics/ campaign/barack-obamas-remarks-to-the-democratic-national.html (accessed February 1, 2021). Compare to Prime Minister Theresa May's statement to the 2016 U.K. Conservative Party conference: "If you believe you're a citizen of the world, you're a citizen of nowhere."

61 John Rawls, *A Theory of Justice* (Cambridge: Harvard University Press, 1971).

gender is no reason for social institutions to favor or disfavor her. Each representative in the original position is therefore deprived of knowledge of the race, class, and gender of the real citizen that they represent. In fact, the veil of ignorance deprives the parties of all facts about citizens that are irrelevant to the choice of principles of justice: not only facts about their race, class, and gender but also facts about their age, natural endowments, and more."[62] Alain Finkielkraut writes, "With the rise of particularism comes the twilight of citizenship as an ideal. The most common tack to take in a society bereft of common beliefs and collective heroism is to turn inward, value the self before all else and, most importantly, to carve out your individual niche."[63]

Identity groups do not seek equal treatment. They seek different treatment. Using the concept of lived experience, they reject groups with different experiences of life and repudiate any attempt to communicate across identities. The concept of cultural appropriation guts the fertile and complex idea of interrelated and interdependent cultures and traditions. By rejecting universalist ideas in favour of tribal loyalty, identity politics, in its drive for dignity and worth, subverts tolerance and promotes prejudice.

Traditional left-wing politics is another casualty of the identity wars. Class struggle is no longer a viable concept. One desperate response of the political left has been to jettison big unifying ideas and rhetoric and move from inclusion and equality to exclusion and division—in other words, to try and coopt the identity politics movement. Another has been to fight back by promoting idealistic concepts of multiculturalism, and a general regard for the dignity of all humanity, which provide for identity groups to respect each other as members of a super-group. "[A] super-group," writes Chua, "does not require its members to shed or suppress their subgroup identities. On the contrary, it allows those subgroup identities to thrive, even as individuals are bound together

---

62 "John Rawls," *Stanford Encyclopedia of Philosophy*, https://plato.stanford.edu/entries/rawls/#OriPos (accessed March 14, 2021).
63 Finkielkraut, note 4, p. 88.

by a strong, overarching collective identity."[64] This seems like a hopeless rearguard action, an impossible attempt to create a universalism that embraces particularism. It is hard to imagine anyone arguing today that the United States, for example, is a super-group where subgroup identities thrive. Kwame Anthony Appiah has observed: "Liberal states depend upon a civic creed that's both potent and lean—potent enough to give significance to citizenship, lean enough to be shared by people with different religious and ethnic affiliations . . . The liberal state's true anthem is: 'We can work it out.'"[65] More lean, than potent, it seems to me. There is much evidence that we can't work it out anymore, if we ever could. But there may be the occasional glimmer of hope. Justin Trudeau has said that Canada, generally regarded as a successful country, could be the world's first postnational state: "There is no core identity, no mainstream in Canada."[66] The strength of Canada is that there is no strong, overarching collective identity. Some might argue that it is also the weakness of Canada.

Is there any chance that antagonistic forces—identity politics and universalism—can be reconciled for the good of all? *The Economist*, an international weekly newspaper published in the United Kingdom, has asked whether France, an idealistic country, "can accommodate more explicit racial identities within its existing model, in ways that neither crush genuinely felt differences nor abandon the colour-blind ideal . . ."[67] The newspaper quoted James Baldwin who said that, when he was in France, he felt free of "the crutches of race." The answer seems

---

64 Chua, note 54, p.12. Chua argues that America is a super-group, unlike, for instance, a country such as France with its political secularism (*laïcité*). She writes of America: "We have forged a national identity that transcends tribal politics—an identity that does not belong to any sub-group, that is strong and capacious enough to hold together an incredibly diverse population . . ." (p. 166).

65 Appiah, note 52, p.103.

66 See Charles Foran, "The Canada Experiment: Is This the World's First 'Postnational' Country? *The Guardian*, January 4, 2017 https://www.theguardian.com/world/2017/jan/04/the-canada-experiment-is-this-the-worlds-first-postnational-country (accessed April 20, 2021).

67 "Colour vision," January 16, 2021, p. 39.

to be (as I discuss later) that France cannot do it. If France can't do it, who can?

JEWS AND IDENTITY POLITICS

What happens to Jews in the turbulent and destructive age of identity politics? How do they assert their identity? How do other identity groups see them?

As for how Jews assert their identity, two trends—one liberal, the other tribal—pull in opposite directions. Writ large, Jews do not look like a modern identity group as I have described it, constantly limiting its characteristics and seeking to exclude from membership those who do not fit an ever-narrowing definition, hostile to those who do not share its identity and therefore cannot understand it. Quite the contrary, in some respects there is more universalism than particularism in the world Jewish community. This is the liberal trend, exemplified by modern self-identification definitions of "Jew."

But some Jews go in a different direction and embrace identity politics. They make many of the complaints and claims that other identity groups make. They express much of the same anger. They burn with a sense of victimhood. They consider their personal worth constantly questioned or denied. An undeniable history of persecution, and particularly the Holocaust, defines them. They claim to be oppressed, marginalized, victimized, and—paradoxically—ignored. They demand dignity, attention, and respect, and do it very effectively. They see antisemitism everywhere. This is the tribal trend.

Identity politics makes Jews more vulnerable, but also gives them an advantage. They are more vulnerable in three ways. First, in an age of particularism, with society no longer held together by universal beliefs, with tolerance for others disappearing, with groups competing for attention, with troubling history readily shoved into the shadows, it is more acceptable and common to criticize and attack anyone who does not share your identity. Criticism and prejudice are simply politics as usual.

And so, antisemitism seems more natural and acceptable, and flourishes more easily, than ever before. Second, identity politics is exclusionary. It accentuates the idea of the Jew as the proverbial Other.[68] It can even summon up and seek to justify the spectre of property expropriation (majorities always want to take property away from minorities). Third, attempted assimilation into the broader community, a long-standing technique of Jewish minorities, is much more difficult in the age of identity politics. Meaningful broad communities that welcome others and ignore distinctions are dying rather than developing.

Mind you, assimilation of Jews into the broader community has seldom been successful. Stefan Zweig wrote, "For Jews, adaptation to the human or national environment in which they lived was not only a measure taken for their own protection, but also a deeply felt private need. Their desire for a homeland, for peace, repose and security, a place where they would not be strangers, impelled them to form a passionate attachment to the culture around them."[69] The passionate attachment was seldom reciprocated. Zweig was writing about Vienna at the beginning of the 20th century, before what he calls the "tragic downfall." Jean-Paul Sartre called assimilation "a dream."[70] The political theorist Hannah Arendt "wanted, above all, for her fellow Jews to abandon the delusion that a disavowal of their Jewishness or the goodwill of other peoples would somehow save them." She called this delusion "worldlessness,"[71] driven by a misplaced and shameful survival instinct that made Jews victims. Pauline Wengeroff, describing her life as a Russian Jew in the 19th century, writes about how Lithuanian Jews in the 1860s and 1870s included "so many men of completely European

---

68 The Other is the opposite of the Self, the societal norm. The Other is socially subordinate, excluded and displaced, disenfranchised, colonially exploited, at the margins of society. The Other is non-white, female, LGBT, a native, an illegal immigrant, a Jew.

69 Zweig, note 27, p. 41.

70 Sartre, note 5, p. 143.

71 See Linfield, note 26, p. 20. Arendt regarded worldlessness as the defining Jewish characteristic.

culture, men whose great achievements in the most diverse fields of literature, science and art, were acknowledged with secular honors and titles."[72] Soon she was describing the pogroms of the 1880s: "First to suffer were the Jews of Kiev, Romny, Konotop and other places. They were helpless before the attacks of the wild masses . . ."[73] Finkielkraut has called assimilation a dreadful misunderstanding. "Genocide was not imposed on the Jews *in spite of* their effort to assimilate, but *in response* to this very attempt. The more they hid their Jewishness, the more terrifying they became to others."[74]

But identity politics offers Jews one advantage. It validates the inclination to strike back when criticized and attacked. Historically, this inclination was often weak and sometimes absent, but now the gloves are off. Jews are magnificently free to behave aggressively as if they were an identity group like any other. Identity politics magnifies defensive reactions. Defence becomes offence. Amy Chua writes, "When groups feel threatened, they retreat into tribalism. They close ranks and become more insular, more defensive, more punitive, more us-versus-them."[75]

There are not many Jews in the world. In every country except Israel they are a very small percentage of the general population. Yet in the countries of the Diaspora the Jewish voice is alive and powerful. Tiny Jewish communities, often feeling on the defensive, propelled, and united by fear of antisemitism, act like a real identity group and attract much attention. They demand it. They are dexterous in advancing their interests. This is even more exceptional when you consider that these communities have fragmented, uncertain, and controversial identities, are far from monolithic in beliefs, attitudes, and aspirations, and often are rife with internal disagreement (see Chapter 2).

---

72 Pauline Wengeroff, *Rememberings: The World of a Russian-Jewish Woman in the Nineteenth Century* (Bethesda: University Press of Maryland), p. 71.
73 Wengeroff, note 72, p. 223.
74 Finkielkraut, note 4, p. 69.
75 Chua, note 54, pp. 8–9.

CHAPTER 2

JEWS IN THE WORLD

LOSSES AND FAREWELLS

The story of Jews in the world is a story of constant movement, of the half-packed suitcase, of the shadow of the Holocaust, of fear and trembling, of the Jewish community dwindling and divided. It is a story of losses and farewells. It is the story of people who wander the world and—so it seems—have always done so.

At the beginning of the 20th century, my father's family lived in Cherkasy, in what is now Ukraine, then part of Russia. Cherkasy is on the eastern bank of the Dnipro River, about 200 kilometres southeast of Kiev. My grandfather, Volodya Slavouski, was born there in 1885. He left as a young man and went to Kiev in search of a better life. In 1907, following a fresh wave of pogroms in Russia, Volodya fled to Berlin with his new wife Manya Brainos. Manya was disguised as a boy for the trip. Later they went to Paris. In 1914, Volodya and Manya moved once more, this time to London. In May 1919, a particularly brutal pogrom took place in Cherkasy, where Volodya's two brothers and his sister still lived. Hundreds of Jews were murdered, and three thousand houses were looted.[76] The three siblings fled Cherkasy and, following a route much-travelled by refugees, went to Odessa, then by boat across the Dniester River to Bucharest, then to Paris, and finally to London to join Volodya, who by then was a successful businessman in the fur trade. One of these brothers moved to Canada in 1935, and, after World War II, one of Volodya and Manya's two sons moved to the United States and the other, my father, to Canada. More distant members of the Slavouski family went at different times to Colombia and other countries in South America. Following the withdrawal of the United Kingdom from the European Union in 2020, some of Volodya and Manya's descendants living in Britain, who had a non-Jewish German father, obtained German citizenship, thinking thereby to protect and enhance their future; the irony did not escape them. This is not an unusual story for a Jewish family across the generations, wandering the world, going back and forth, packing and unpacking, seeking safe haven and a better future, shuffling allegiances, always on the look-out.

Jews have always been on the move, restless, nomads by necessity, roaming across countries and continents, thinking of the next place to go, a place where they may be welcome and not in danger, a place free of antisemitism and persecution.[77] The allure of Israel has been that it seems to offer an alternative to that history of wandering, as intended by Zionism. As we shall see later, it is a problematic alternative. Today, the patterns of the past continue, if somewhat attenuated. French Jews move to Britain, Israel, and Canada; British Jews move to France and Germany; Israeli Jews move to Germany and Canada; South African Jews move to Israel; Russian Jews move to the United States and Britain;

---

76 Jeffrey Veidlinger, *In the Midst of Civilized Europe: The Pogroms of 1918–1921 and the Onset of the Holocaust* (Toronto: HarperCollins, 2021), p. 196.

77 Not all wandering involved crossing borders. Jeffrey Veidlinger, writing about Soviet Ukraine in the 1920s, notes that "most Jews fled internally, migrating from one town to another, hoping to find solace and opportunity without abandoning the land that was all they had ever known." See Jeffrey Veidlinger, *In the Shadow of the Shtetl: Small-Town Jewish Life in Soviet Ukraine* (Bloomington: Indiana University Press, 2016), p. 38.

Ukrainian Jews go wherever they can; U.S. Jews move to Israel. Jews have sometimes been called "rootless cosmopolitans" (the epithet was a favourite of the Soviets). This implies that Jews have little commitment to whatever country they live in and are rightfully an object of national suspicion. Here is a deep paradox, for Jews in history are always searching for place, desperate to belong, to not be rootless, to find a home.

Stefan Zweig wrote in 1942, shortly before he committed suicide in Brazil: "For many years I thought that my deliberate training of myself to feel that everything was temporary was a flaw in me, but later on, when I was forced time and again to leave every home I made for myself and saw everything around me fall apart, that mysterious lifelong sensation of not being tied down was helpful. It was a lesson I learnt early, and it has made loss and farewells easier for me."[78] Zweig described a scene he saw in a London travel agency before he left for Brazil: "It was full of refugees, nearly all of them Jewish, and they all wanted to go somewhere, anywhere. It didn't matter what country, they would have gone to the ice of the North Pole or the blazing sands of the Sahara just to get away, move on . . ."[79] In his suicide note, addressed to the president of the PEN club of Brazil, Zweig spoke of "my spiritual home, Europe, having destroyed itself . . . my energy is exhausted by long years of peregrination as one without a country."[80] He and his wife had spent years on the move—Ostend, Zurich, Calcutta, London, Bath, Moscow, Ossining (a suburb of New York City, home of John Cheever, and of Don Draper, the fictional hero of *Mad Men*), Rio, Buenos Aires, Petrópolis, other places. A friend of Zweig said, "no matter where you

78 Zweig, note 27.
79 Zweig, note 27, p. 452.
80 "Stefan Zweig, Wife End Lives in Brazil," *The New York Times*, February 24, 1942 https://timesmachine.nytimes.com/timesmachine/1942/02/24/85274374. html?pageNumber=1 (accessed December 20, 2020). And see Robert Philpot, "Diaries Show Literary Giant Stefan Zweig's iInner Turmoil as Nazis Stormed Europe," *The Times of Israel*, October 25, 2021 https://www.timesofisrael.com/ diaries-show-literary-giant-stefan-zweigs-inner-turmoil-as-nazis-stormed-europe/ (accessed October 28, 2021).

met Zweig, his manner suggested a half-packed suitcase in the next room."[81]

DWINDLING AND DIVIDED

In 1939 there were about 16.5 million Jews in the world. There were 11 million in 1945. This dramatic decline needs no explanation. At the beginning of 2018, the world Jewish population was about 14.6 million.[82] In 2021 it was estimated to have grown to about 15.2 million.[83] There may never again be as many Jews in the world as there were in 1939. James Carroll has observed: "Jews accounted for 10 percent of the total population of the Roman Empire. By that ratio, if other factors had not intervened, there would be 200 million Jews in the world today . . ."[84]

Three Jewish demographic trends have prevailed since 1945. First, the number of Jews as a proportion of the world's population has decreased substantially. Second, the number of Jews living in what is now Israel has increased dramatically. Third, the number of Jews living outside Israel has decreased significantly. DellaPergola writes:

> Israel's Jewish population increased linearly from an initial one-half million in 1945 and 630,000 in 1948 to over 6.5 million in 2018. The Jewish population of the Diaspora, from an initial 10.5 million in 1945, was quite stable in number until the early 1970s, when it started decreasing to less than 8.1 million in 2018. The world's total

---

81 See Leo Carey, "The Escape Artist," *The New Yorker*, August 20, 2012 https://www.newyorker.com/magazine/2012/08/27/the-escape-artist-3 (accessed December 20, 2020).

82 Sergio DellaPergola, note 9, pp. 10–11. These numbers refer to members of DellaPergola's "core" Jewish population, people who consider Judaism their exclusive identity. See Chapter 1.

83 See "Jewish Population Rises to 15.2m Worldwide," *Hamodia*, September 5, 2021 https://hamodia.com/2021/09/05/jewish-population-rises-15-2m-worldwide/ (accessed September 26, 2021).

84 Carroll, note 2, p. 26.

population increased more than threefold from 2.315 billion in 1945 to 7.536 billion by mid-2017. Thus, the relative share of Jews among the world's total population steadily diminished from 4.75 per 1,000 in 1945 to 1.94 per 1,000 currently—or one per every 515 inhabitants in the world.[85]

Today, the Jews of Israel and the United States make up about 84 per cent of the world Jewish population. About 45 per cent of the world's Jews, almost seven million, live in Israel. Some 39 per cent live in the United States. France, England, Germany, South Africa, and Canada account for almost all the rest.[86] The once great European Jewish community has largely disappeared, its members murdered, or driven elsewhere by Russian pogroms, by the Holocaust, and by other persecution. Many have been lured by the promise of Israel. In the latter part of the 19th century, European Jews represented 88 per cent of the world's Jews, most of them living in Eastern Europe. A Russian census of 1897 counted more than five million Jews, half the entire world Jewish population of that time. In 1945, European Jews accounted for about 35 per cent of the total Jewish population. By 2020, they made up only 9 per cent of world Jewry.[87] DellaPergola and Staetsky comment: "[T]he proportion of Jews residing in Europe is about the same as it was at the time of the first Jewish global population account conducted by Benjamin of Tudela, a Jewish medieval traveler, in 1170."[88]

A survey of the world's principal Jewish communities tells us several things. Constant historical migration of Jews, in many directions, has created diversity and lack of cohesion. Jews are not bound together

---

85 DellaPergola, note 9, p. 5.
86 Ilan Stavans makes the point that the Jews of Latin America "as a conglomerate . . . represent the third-largest concentration of Jews worldwide, after the United States and Israel and before France and Canada." See Stavans, *The Seventh Heaven: Travels Through Jewish Latin America* (Pittsburgh: University of Pittsburgh Press, 2020), p. 7.
87 See note 9.
88 Note 9, p. 13.

by religion, ethnicity, politics, or even an overarching commitment to Israel. International Jewry is an imagined community.

ISRAEL

The State of Israel contains almost half the world's Jews. They or their ancestors came from Europe (particularly the Soviet Union), Africa (particularly Morocco), and Asia. There were two major waves of immigration, the first between 1948 and 1951 when about 700,000 Jewish refugees arrived (500,000 of them Sephardic Jews from Muslim lands), and the second, over a million immigrants, from post-Soviet states after the collapse of the Soviet Union in 1991 (these are sometimes called the "Russian Israelis").

The Israeli Jewish community is diverse and splintered. There is a wide range of cultural traditions, religious commitment, and religious practices. This has been true from the beginning. Immigrant Jews from Muslim lands (the Sephardi), who spoke Arabic and had an Arabic culture, and those from Europe (the Ashkenazi), had little mutual regard and almost nothing in common. The Ashkenazi thought the Sephardi were socially and culturally inferior and "fit mainly for manual labour and domestic service."[89] European Jews thought it was more appropriate to use Sephardi rather than Palestinian Arabs as a source of labour. The Israeli authorities and Israeli institutions regarded Arab-Jewish immigrants "with varying degrees of deep contempt and manifest suspicion."[90] David Ben Gurion, the first prime minister of Israel, regarded "the infusion of 'oriental' tendencies into Israel culture, as a corrupting force."[91] In 1983, the scholar Bernard Lewis described Israel as place "where the two great branches of the Jewish

---

89 Martin Gilbert, *In Ishmael's House* (Toronto: McClelland and Stewart, 2010), p. 311.
90 Sand, note 29, p. 45.
91 Deborah A. Starr and Sasson Somekh, introduction to Jacqueline Shohet Kahanoff, *Mongrels or Marvels* (Stanford: Stanford University Press, 2011), pp. xxiii–xxiv.

people, the Jews of Islam and the Jews of Christendom, are meeting again for the first time in centuries and are struggling to create a new synthesis based on their common Jewishness. Their encounter repeats in miniature the clash of the two civilizations from which they come, and the aim of unity will not easily be achieved."[92] But the ground has since shifted. Walter Russell Mead has observed that the Ashkenazi ascendancy has weakened considerably in recent times: "The old Israeli establishment held on in institutions like the judiciary, the universities, and certain institutions in the security field, but its members were increasingly alienated from the less polished, less western, less liberal, more religious, and more Middle Eastern country into which Israel is changing."[93]

Theodor Herzl, the founder of Zionism, wrote, long before the creation of Israel: "If the Jews ever 'returned home' one day, they would discover on the next that they do not belong together. For centuries they have been rooted in diverse nationalisms; they differ from each other, group by group. The only thing they have in common is the pressure holding them together."[94] The Jewish Romanian novelist Mikhail Sebastian asked, writing in the 1930s, "One day—who knows—we may make peace with the anti-Semites. But when will we make peace with ourselves?"[95] In 2021 Patrick Kingsley of *The New York Times* made a trip across Israel with photojournalist Laetitia Vancon. He reported: "We found a country still wrestling with contradictions left unresolved at its birth, and with the consequences of its occupation of the West Bank and Gaza in 1967. We found a people facing complex questions

---

92 *The Jews of Islam* (Princeton: Princeton University Press, 1984), p. xi. See also Lyn Julius, *Uprooted: How 3000 Years of Jewish Civilization in the Arab World Vanished Overnight* (Chicago: Valentine Mitchell, 2018), chapter 9 ("Mizrahi Wars of Politics and Culture").

93 Walter Russell Mead, *The Arc of a Covenant* (New York: Walter A. Knopf, 2022), p. 545.

94 Quoted by Milton Viorst, *Zionism: The Birth and Transformation of an Ideal* (New York: Thomas Dunne Books, 2016), p. 253.

95 Mihail Sebastian, *For Two Thousand Years* (London: Penguin Classics, 2016), p. 43. This book was first published in 1934 as *De douä mii de ani*.

about what it means to be Israeli, or a Palestinian citizen of Israel. And we found a battle of narratives — waged not only between Jews and Arabs, but also among Jews themselves. Israel's founders hoped to create a melting pot, a society that blended diverse communities into a single Jewish state. But we encountered an Israel that at times felt more like an unsolvable jigsaw puzzle — a collection of incompatible factions, each with its own priorities, grievances and history."[96] Some say there remains a pervasive racism in Israel towards Sephardic Jews. A 2021 film—*The Forgotten Ones*—by French-Israeli filmmaker Michale Boganim explores this subject. Says Boganim about Sephardic Jews, following a recent trip across Israel: "When I met these young people who live in Israeli projects I realized that what they're going through, the way they have channeled that rage and developed an underground culture is similar to what children of immigrants are doing in many countries around the world, for instance in the U.S. or France. This is when I realized how universal the immigrant experience is."[97]

A 2016 Pew Research Center survey[98] found deep divisions in contemporary Israeli society, not only between Israeli Jews and the Arab minority (about 20 per cent of the population) but also among Jewish religious subgroups. The Pew Research Centre reports: "These divisions are reflected in starkly contrasting positions on many public policy questions, including marriage, divorce, religious conversion, military conscription, gender segregation and public transportation. Overwhelmingly, Haredi and Dati Jews (both generally considered highly

96 Patrick Kingsley and Laetitia Vancon, "Whose Promised Land? A Journey into a Divided Israel," *The New York Times*, October 25, 2021 https://www. nytimes.com/2021/10/25/world/middleeast/israel-jews-palestinians-journey. html?referringSource=articleShare (accessed November 25, 2021).

97 Elsa Keslassy, "Michael Boganim Discusses Venice-Bound Documentary 'The Forgotten Ones' About Discrimination of Oriental Jew in Israel," *Variety*, September 5, 2021 https://variety.com/2021/film/global/michale-boganim-venice-the-forgotten-ones-1235056832/ (accessed October 21, 2021).

98 "Israel's Religiously Divided Society," March 8, 2016 https://www.pewforum. org/2016/03/08/israels-religiously-divided-society/ (accessed January 25, 2021).

religious) express the view that Israel's government should promote religious beliefs and values, while secular Jews strongly favor separation of religion from government policy."[99] Nearly all Israeli Jews identify as one of Haredi (ultra-Orthodox), Dati (religious), Masorti (traditional), or Hiloni (secular). In 2016 the Haridim accounted for 9 per cent of the Jewish population (since then the percentage has increased to about 12 per cent[100] and it continues to increase at a rapid pace); Datiim, 13 per cent; Masortim, 29 per cent; and Hilonim, 49 per cent. Most Haredim oppose Zionism, maintaining that Judaism is a religion that should not be dependent on a country and that only the Messiah can establish a Jewish state. Some Haredim support the Islamist Raam party on the grounds that Arab lawmakers are less likely to promote secularism and are conservative in general, opposing—for example—gay rights. During the COVID-19 pandemic of 2020–2022, the differences between highly religious and secular Jews were starkly illustrated, with the ultra-Orthodox resisting lockdown, sometimes violently, on the grounds that it prevented them from properly practising their religion.[101]

And then there is the familiar general ambivalence over Jewish identity. The 2016 Pew survey reported, "Most of the ultra-Orthodox say 'being Jewish' is mainly a matter of religion, while secular Jews tend to say it is mainly a matter of ancestry and/or culture."[102] As for antisemitism, the Pew survey said: "Israeli Jews all but universally say anti-Semitism is at least somewhat common around the world today, including nearly two-thirds who say it is very common. And roughly three-quarters say anti-Semitism is not only common but on the rise globally, while virtually no Israeli Jews say it is decreasing."[103]

---

99 Pew, note 98, p. 5.
100 See The Israel Democracy Institute, *2019 Statistical Report on Ultra-Orthodox Society in Israel*, https://en.idi.org.il/articles/29348 (accessed March 1, 2021).
101 See Ronen Bergman, "How the Pandemic Nearly Tore Israel Apart," *The New York Times*, February 25, 2021 https://www.nytimes.com/2021/02/25/magazine/how-the-pandemic-nearly-tore-israel-apart.html?referringSource=articleShare (accessed March 1, 2021).
102 Pew, note 98, p. 6.
103 Pew, note 98, p. 221.

Despite profound differences and disagreements on many matters among Israel's Jews, it would be a mistake to think that lack of cohesiveness in Israel is the entire story and explains everything. Rashid Khalidi has written about the Palestinian "fatally flawed analysis of Israel as a deeply divided and 'artificial' polity, which ignores the manifestly successful nation-building efforts of Zionism over more than a century, as well as the cohesiveness of Israel society in spite of its many internal divisions."[104] The Palestinians, facing a regional superpower always ready to flex its economic and military muscles, have paid dearly for this flawed analysis.

THE UNITED STATES

The modern American Jewish community began with the immigration of some three million Jews as part of the great exodus from Russia in the late 19th and early 20th centuries. Most of these refugees settled in New York City. Further substantial Jewish immigration occurred in the years after World War II, following relaxation of U.S. restrictive immigration laws and quotas and the lifting by Mikhail Gorbachev in 1989 of limits on emigration from the Soviet Union. There are now, by some estimates, as many as 7.6 million American Jews, broadly defined, comprising about 2.4 per cent of the American population.[105] The number depends on who you consider to be a Jew, which, as we have seen, is an imprecise subject of continuing debate. Some place the U.S. Jewish population at closer to 6 million.

It is not Judaism that binds American Jews together. A 2013 Pew Research Center portrait of Jewish Americans[106] found that 22 per cent

104 Rashid Khalidi, *The Hundred Years' War on Palestine: A History of Settler Colonialism and Resistance, 1917-2017* (New York: Picador, 2020), p. 216.
105 See Steinhardt Social Research Institute American Jewish Population Project, "US Jewish Population Estimates 2020," https://ajpp.brandeis.edu/us_jewish_population_2020 (accessed 24 March 24, 2021).
106 Pew Research Center, *A Portrait of Jewish Americans: Findings from a Pew*

describe themselves as having no religion at all. Indeed, American Jews are considerably less religious than the general public of the United States. The 2013 Pew portrait reports, "Secularism has a long tradition in Jewish life in America, and most U.S. Jews seem to recognize this: 62% say being Jewish is mainly a matter of ancestry and culture, while just 15% say it is mainly a matter of religion."[107] Seven years later, a new Pew study on Jewish Americans reported much the same: "Overall, about a quarter of U.S. Jewish adults (27%) do not identify with the Jewish religion: They consider themselves to be Jewish ethnically, culturally, or by family background and have a Jewish parent or were raised Jewish, but they answer a question about their current *religion* by describing themselves as atheist, agnostic or 'nothing in particular' rather than as Jewish. Among Jewish adults under 30, four-in-ten describe themselves this way."[108]

Most American Jews declare an emotional attachment to Israel, albeit a vague one. The 2020 Pew report found that 82 per cent of U.S. Jews say caring about Israel is either "essential" or "important" to what being Jewish means to them. But there is some evidence that this attachment is becoming weaker, particularly among younger Jews. This weakening may in part be a result of controversial Israeli national and international policies and in particular the handling by the Israeli government of

Research Center Survey of U.S. Jews, October 1, 2013 https://www.pewresearch. org/wp-content/uploads/sites/7/2013/10/jewish-american-full-report-for-web. pdf (accessed January 21, 2021). A projection based on the 2013 Pew study, published in 2021, predicts "that over the next 50 years, the demographics of U.S. Jews are likely to change dramatically, with the share of the population that is Orthodox rising from 12 percent to 29 percent, with their share of the child population increasing from 22 percent to 51 percent." See Edieal J. Pinker, "Projecting Religious Demographics: The Case of Jews in the United States," *Journal for the Scientific Study of Religion*, March 5, 2021 https://onlinelibrary. wiley.com/doi/abs/10.1111/jssr.12716 (accessed May 6, 2021).

107 Pew, note 106, p. 8.
108 Pew Research Center, *Jewish Americans in 2020*, May 11, 2021 https://www. pewforum.org/2021/05/11/jewish-americans-in-2020/ (accessed May 12, 2021). The 2020 study showed little change from the conclusions of the 2013 study.

the Palestinian issue.[109] Increasingly some American Jews seem willing to refer to Israel as a human rights violator because of the way the state treats Palestinians. The American academic Saree Makdisi, who is of Palestinian background, has argued that the conflict between Zionism and Palestinians has been reframed in recent times; he writes that it is now seen as "a confrontation between a people demanding equality and rights and a state representing gross inequality."[110] This shift in perspective, says Makdisi, means that the global basis for the support of Israel has shifted from the left to the right. The violence between Israel and Hamas in May 2021, in the context of domestic turmoil in America around issues of racial and social injustice, further strained loyalty to Israel and produced an "identity crisis" among some American Jews, particularly young ones.[111] In May 2021, 93 young American rabbinical and cantorial students drafted a controversial open letter,[112] which urged Jews to rethink their support for American

---

109 See Dov Waxman, *Trouble in the Tribe: The American Jewish Conflict over Israel* (Princeton: Princeton University Press, 2016). A 2022 Pew Research Center survey found that Americans under the age of 30 view the Palestinian people at least as warmly as the Israeli people and rate the Palestinian government as favourably as the Israeli government. See Becka A. Alper, "Modest Warming in U.S. Views on Israel and Palestinians," Pew Research Center, May 26, 2022 https://www.pewresearch.org/religion/2022/05/26/modest-warming-in-u-s-views-on-israel-and-palestinians/ (accessed June 4, 2022).

110 Saree Makdisi, *Tolerance Is a Wasteland: Palestine and the Culture of Denial* (Oakland: University of California Press, 2022), p.145. This pro-Palestinian anti-Israel book is powerfully argued but is undermined by intemperance.

111 See Elizabeth Dias and Ruth Graham, "Gaza Conflict Stokes 'Identity Crisis' for Young American Jews," *The New York Times*, May 20, 2021 https://www.nytimes.com/2021/05/19/us/jews-israel-palestine.html?referringSource=articleShare (accessed May 20, 2021). And see Allan C. Brownfeld, "Israel's Nature Increasingly Alienates American Jews," *Washington Report on Middle East Affairs*, September 8, 2021 https://www.wrmea.org/israel-palestine/israels-nature-increasingly-alienates-american-jews.html (accessed October 21, 2021), and Philip Weiss, "U.S. Jews Favor Return to Iran Deal, and Don't Care About Israel as a Political Issue," *Mondoweiss*, April 14, 2022 https://mondoweiss.net/2022/04/u-s-jews-favor-return-to-iran-deal-and-dont-care-about-israel-as-a-political-issue/ (accessed April 20, 2022).

112 https://docs.google.com/document/d/17iNzy0uThn6YECqiBx9t_R-WAHF7m2 Kkxxiq8v0IfPA/edit (accessed November 5, 2021). This letter raised the ire of

military aid to Israel; compared the Palestinians' plight to that of Black Americans; described Israel's two separate legal systems as "apartheid"; and "insisted that Jewish educators complicate their teaching of Israel's founding to convey 'the messy truth of a persecuted people searching for safety, going to a land full of meaning for the Jewish people, full of meaning for so many other peoples, and also full of human beings who didn't ask for new neighbors.'"[113]

The 2020 Pew study reported that 45 per cent of U.S. Jews think there is a lot of antisemitism in the United States. Seventy-five per cent says there is more than there was five years ago. A different 2020 survey found that 88 per cent of American Jews thought antisemitism was a problem in the United States, and 82 per cent thought that it had increased over the past five years, although a big majority of those surveyed said they had not been the target of an antisemitic physical attack or remark.[114] One 2021 poll reported that 40 per cent of Jewish Americans had heard antisemitic comments, slurs or threats directed at someone else over the last twelve months, and 63 per cent had experienced or witnessed some form of antisemitic incident over the past five years.[115] Another 2021 poll, conducted on behalf of the American Jewish Committee, reported that 90 per cent of American Jews thought that antisemitism

many Jews. Jonathan Tobin of the Jewish News Syndicate, in a general attack on the coverage of Israel by *The New York Times*, described the letter as "a disgraceful and self-important rant filled with virtue signaling and pseudo-religious contempt for Israel that displayed the signers' tunnel vision about the conflict and lack of understanding of the dilemmas faced by the Israeli people." See "Anti-Israel Bias in One of America's Biggest Newspapers Matters," November 4, 2021, https://www.jns.org/opinion/anti-israel-bias-in-one-of-americas-biggest-newspapers-matters/ (accessed November 6, 2021).

113 Marc Tracy, "Inside the Unraveling of American Zionism," *The New York Times*, November 2, 2021 https://www.nytimes.com/2021/11/02/magazine/israel-american-jews.html (accessed November 5, 2021).

114 American Jewish Committee, *The State of Antisemitism in America 2020: AJC's Survey of American Jews* https://www.ajc.org/AntisemitismReport2020/Survey-of-American-Jews (accessed January 21, 2021).

115 ADL, "2021 Survey on Jewish Americans' Experiences with Antisemitism," March 31, 2021 https://www.adl.org/blog/2021-survey-on-jewish-americans-experiences-with-antisemitism (accessed April 2, 2021).

was "a very serious problem" or "somewhat of a problem," and 82 per cent considered that over the past five years antisemitism in the United States had "increased a lot" or "increased somewhat." Ninety-seven per cent reported in this poll that over the past twelve months they had not been the target of an antisemitic physical attack and 83 per cent had not been the target of an antisemitic remark in person.[116] The journalist Laura Adkins has pointed out that this poll result implies that 3 per cent of American Jews, or close to 200,000 people, *were* physically attacked. This conclusion, says Adkins, is "impossible-to-fathom." Says Adkins: "Any low single-digit survey result is suspect because it might fall within the margin of error — as in this case, since the margin in the AJC survey is 3.9%. That means if the survey were repeated many times, the 'yes' answer to this particular question would likely range from zero to 6.9%." Adkins continues, as part of a devastating critique of polls of this kind, the results of which are widely quoted and used for many political purposes but should be suspect, "Groups that commission these surveys often stand to benefit from depicting antisemitism as a growing and urgent problem; fear-mongering makes for good fundraising."[117] Both the 2013 and 2020 Pew surveys found that Jewish Americans think there is as much—or more—discrimination in U.S. society against groups other than Jews, including Muslim, Black, Hispanic, and gay or lesbian Americans.

---

116 *The State of Antisemitism in America 2021: AJC's Survey of American Jews* October 2021 https://www.ajc.org/AntisemitismReport2021/AmericanJews (accessed October 27, 2021).

117 Laura E. Adkins, "How to Lie with Statistics, Antisemitism Edition," *Forward*, October 27, 2021 https://forward.com/opinion/477225/ajc-survey-antisemitism-anti-zionism-islamophobia/ (accessed October 28, 2021).

FRANCE

Modern France rejects identity politics and explicitly favours universalism over particularism, at least in theory. The universalist model rejects multiculturalism and "assumes that all citizens have equal rights as individuals, not groups."[118] There are about 450,000 Jews in France, the largest Jewish community in Europe (the precise number is unknown, since, in keeping with universalism, the French census does not ask about ethnic or religious identity). This is less than 1 per cent of France's overall population and only 3 per cent of the world's tiny Jewish population.

In February 2019, I was staying in an apartment on Ile Saint-Louis in central Paris. On the outside of the apartment building was a plaque: "A la memoire des 112 habitants de cette maison dont 40 petits enfants déportés et mort dans les camps Allemands en 1942." There was a Jewish-owned restaurant around the corner from this building. One morning "JUDEN" was scrawled in yellow paint across the shop window. This was one of many similar events in France at the time. Much of the French Jewish community has felt under siege because of sporadic incidents—some violent—of this kind. French officialdom recognizes Jewish apprehensions and responds with Gallic rhetoric. In February 2019, France's then interior minister, Christophe Castaner, said "Antisemitism is spreading like poison."[119] President Emmanuel Macron spoke of a "resurgence of anti-Semitism unseen since World War II," which, he said, is not only happening in France but in "all of Europe and most Western democracies."[120] Polls show that a majority

118 "Colour Vision," *The Economist*, January 16, 2021, pp. 38–39.
119 Angelique Chrisafis, "'Spreading Like Poison': Flurry of Antisemitic Acts Alarms France," *The Guardian*, February 12, 2019 https://www.theguardian.com/world/2019/feb/12/french-police-investigate-antisemitic-attacks-in-paris-simone-veil (accessed December 15, 2020).
120 Saskya Vandoorne, Lindsay Isaac, and Tara John, "Macron Says Anti-Semitism Is at Worst Levels Since World War Two," CNN, February 21, 2019 https://www.cnn.com/2019/02/21/europe/macron-anti-semitism-france-crackdown-intl/index.html (accessed December 15, 2020).

of French Jews, perhaps prompted by overreaching and alarmist official statements made for political reasons, are nervous and periodically consider leaving the country. Some actually do leave, most going to Israel (encouraged to do so by the Israeli government), others to Britain or Canada. But the extent of antisemitism in the general French population can be easily exaggerated. A 2017 Pew Research Center survey "found that a majority of French adults reject negative Jewish stereotypes and express an accepting attitude towards Jews."[121] This fact is often drowned out by reflex cries of alarm and despair from France's Jewish community.

Hanging over the country still, colouring everything, is the treatment during World War II of French Jews in occupied France, metropolitan Vichy France, and in Vichy-controlled French North Africa. It is estimated that about 75,000 Jews were rounded up by the Germans, with the enthusiastic help of the French authorities, and deported to concentration camps. Only about 3,000 of these survived. On July 16, 1995, the 53rd anniversary of the first mass arrest of Jews in Paris (the infamous Vél d'Hiv roundup), French President Jacques Chirac acknowledged French guilt: "These dark hours forever sully our history and are an insult to our past and our traditions. Yes, the criminal folly of the occupiers was seconded by the French, by the French state . . . France, the homeland of the Enlightenment and of the rights of man, a land of welcome and asylum, on that day committed the irreparable. Breaking its word, it handed those who were under its protection over to their executioners."[122] On July 16, 2022, the 80th anniversary of Vél d'Hiv, President Emmanuel Macron said of the

---

121 See Jeff Diamant, "Negative Stereotypes About Jews Largely Rejected in France," Factank, March 13, 2019 https://www.pewresearch.org/fact-tank/2019/03/13/negative-stereotypes-about-jews-are-largely-rejected-in-france/ (accessed December 19, 2020).

122 For a balanced view of France and the Holocaust, see Susan Zuccotti, *The Holocaust, the French, and the Jews* (New York: Basic Books, 1993). An excellent account of Vichy, and the Jewish situation in France since then, is Daniel Solomon, "A Legend of Innocence," *Tablet* June 28, 2022 https://www.tabletmag.com/sections/arts-letters/articles/legend-innocence-france (accessed July 12, 2022).

roundup, "The French state deliberately failed in all the duties of the homeland of the Enlightenment and of human rights."

Two strains of antisemitism have converged in modern France, each feeding the other. One is rooted in a history the like of which does not exist in any other major national Jewish community. The most famous expression of this history was the decade-long Dreyfus Affair, which began in December 1894 with the trial and conviction for treason of Captain Alfred Dreyfus, a Jewish army officer.[123] The Austrian-Hungarian journalist Theodor Herzl was present in the courtyard of the École militaire in Paris when, at nine in the morning on January 5, 1895, following Dreyfus's conviction, the epaulettes were torn from his uniform in an appalling way designed for maximum humiliation. This was the so-called "degradation ceremony." Herzl went on to become the father of modern Zionism and the leading exponent of Jewish immigration to Palestine (see Chapter 5). Stefan Zweig, who knew Herzl in Vienna, wrote of Herzl's reaction to the degradation of Dreyfus: "He had seen the epaulettes torn from the pale man's uniform as he cried out aloud, 'I am innocent.' And he had known in his heart at that moment that Dreyfus was indeed innocent, and only the fact that he was Jewish had brought the terrible suspicion of treason down on him."[124] After professing his innocence, Dreyfus unaccountably shouted, "Vive la France!"

---

123 The complex Dreyfus affair has been written about extensively. See, for example, Louis Begley, *Why the Dreyfus Affair Matters* (New Haven: Yale University Press, 2010). Adam Gopnik writes, in reviewing Begley's book: "The Dreyfus affair was the first indication that a new epoch of progress and cosmopolitan optimism would be met by a countervailing wave of hatred that deformed the next half century of European history ... [The Dreyfus Affair] showed that a huge number of Europeans, in a time largely smiling and prosperous, liked engaging in raw, animal religious hatred, and only felt fully alive when they did. Hatred and bigotry were not a vestige of the superstitious past but a living fire—just what comes, and burns, naturally." "Trial of the Century," *The New Yorker*, September 21, 2009 https://www.newyorker.com/magazine/2009/09/28/trial-of-the-century (accessed December 14, 2020). And see Ruth Harris for a particularly convincing and insightful account: *Dreyfus: Politics, Emotion, and the Scandal of the Century* (New York: Picador, 2010).

124 Zweig, note 27, p. 124. Some scholars claim that Herzl believed Dreyfus to be guilty but used the affair to create support for his Zionist goals.

Dreyfus spent five years of solitary confinement in dreadful conditions on the French penal colony of Devil's Island.[125] After long and complex legal proceedings, he was finally declared innocent in 1906 by the Court of Cassation, the highest court of appeal in France. Then—extraordinarily—Dreyfus rejoined the French army, his devotion to France apparently undimmed by his persecution and imprisonment. He was promoted to the rank of major and made a knight of the Legion of Honour. During all these years, and afterwards, the Dreyfus Affair roiled France. James Carroll writes that it stands "as a marker of the fact that Catholic antisemitism was alive and well, armed and dangerous . . . at the crucial modern moment. An expressly Catholic antisemitism was a seedbed for the coming catastrophe."[126] In the 21st century, the Dreyfus Affair is still a source of fascination and political conflict. Dreyfus is buried in Montparnasse Cemetery in Paris. I visited him there. His unremarkable grave is hard to find in the crowded graveyard. The inscription on his tomb records that his granddaughter, Madeline Lévy, was murdered in Auschwitz.

French antisemitism, of course, predated Dreyfus. It has been called France's oldest hatred. Voltaire, Diderot, and others of the *philosophes* famously criticized Jews in the 17th and 18th centuries, although the nature of this criticism can be distorted and exaggerated.[127] After all, the *philosophes* sought to liberate the human mind from any and all religion. Two years after the French revolution of 1789 Jews were allowed to become citizens, but only after extensive and bitter debate; their emancipation itself provoked an antisemitic response. Many antisemitic books, some best sellers, were published in France in the 19th century. Best known is Edouard Drumont's 1886 *La France juive*, 1,200 pages long, which sold 100,000 copies when it was first published

---

125 Described in heart-breaking fashion by Dreyfus himself: *Five Years of My Life, 1894–1899* (Berlin: Comino Verlag, 2019), first published as *Cinq années de ma vie*, in France in 1901.

126 Carroll, note 2, p. 465.

127 See David Nirenberg, note 14, pp. 343–60.

and was reprinted more than 200 times. But French antisemitism at this time was about more than French Jewry. David Remnick has written that in France, by the 19th century, "hatred of Jews was a proxy for a generalized revulsion for modernity, secularism, and republican values."[128] The response of French Jewry to this antisemitism was ill-judged, employing the doomed assimilation strategy. The novelist Louis Begley has written that French Jews "transformed their sense of gratitude for their citizenship into an unswerving patriotism and self-identification with France," which led to "the tendency of French Jews to minimize the importance of anti-Semitism, remain passive, and avoid speaking out against outrageous behaviour . . ."[129] Attempts to assimilate into French society did not prevent deportation to Germany during the Nazi period.

The second strain of French antisemitism was born of post-World War II immigration of Muslims to France, mostly in the 1950s and 1960s and largely from former French colonies in North Africa. Today, Muslim immigrants comprise about 10 per cent of France's population, vastly outnumbering French Jews. Ironically many of the Jews in France today also came from North Africa in the 1950s and 1960s (about 300,000, most from Algeria), spoke Arabic, and at one time were comfortable with their Muslim neighbours with whom they shared some cultural traditions and religious practices. In the early days of their arrival, Jews and Muslims could be found living together in a friendly way in places like Sarcelles or Belleville in the northern suburbs of Paris. This fabric of peace was soon torn. For one thing, as Maud Mandel describes, "While Muslim immigrants were trapped

---

128 "The Shadow of Anti-Semitism in France," *The New Yorker*, January 13, 2015 https://www.newyorker.com/news/daily-comment/shadow-anti-semitism-france (accessed December 14, 2020). It has been argued by some scholars that political antisemitism was a way of rejecting a liberalism that benefitted the Jewish population. Paradoxically, growth of liberal democracy made it easier for antisemitic movements to grow and flourish. With liberalism, Jews were both winners and losers.

129 Begley, note 123, pp. 72–73.

in a cycle of poverty passed on to their children, Jewish migrants experienced a much more rapid social ascent aided, in part, by a more favorable welcome by French authorities . . ."[130] The 1967 war between Israel and its Arab neighbours created new political tensions between Jews and Arabs in France (exemplified by the 1968 Belleville riots), although Mandel argues that the effect of Middle East conflict on relations between French Jews and Muslims can easily be exaggerated and that local and national issues and trends—economic and social inequities between the two communities in particular—were at least as important. There is, it seems, in the world of antisemitism, exaggeration everywhere and on every point.

And then came identity politics, the penetration of particularism, to a country philosophically and politically committed to universalism. A deadly struggle began. "Nineteen-eighties France," says Mandel, "saw an unprecedented rise of identity politics in a nation that had long subsumed cultural, linguistic, and religious diversity in the wider national project."[131] This wider national project began dying a protracted death. Mandel writes, "[W]ell before 2000, French Muslim youth had begun identifying with the Palestinian cause as a way to express their own social frustrations. For those who feel marginalized and disenfranchised in France's poor urban neighborhoods, the Palestinian struggle for recognition has taken on symbolic meaning, allowing anger at Israel to become increasingly entangled with anti-Jewish stereotypes."[132] Francis Fukuyama has observed that following the 1979 Iranian Revolution "Islamist groups began to appear in Europe that argued that Muslims should not seek to integrate, but should maintain separate cultural institutions . . . In France, Muslims became the new proletariat, with part of the left abandoning its traditional secularism in the name of cultural pluralism. Criticism that Islamists

---

130 Maud Mandel, *Muslims and Jews in France: History of a Conflict* (Princeton: Princeton University Press, 2014), p. 154.
131 Note 130, p. 127.
132 Note 130, p. 153.

were themselves intolerant and illiberal were often downplayed under the banner of antiracism and countering Islamophobia."[133]

The rise of Islamist identity politics, associated with terrorist tragedies, frightened a French government dedicated to secularism and universalism, and forced it to move to the right, talking of protecting national identity, in a damaging attempt to retain power. In an ironic twist of fate, following mass immigration of Arabs from France's former colonies, antisemitism has been to some degree replaced by anti-Arab racism, espoused particularly by politicians on the far-right, such as the 2022 failed French presidential candidate Éric Zemmour, a Jew of Algerian origin. Mitchell Abidor and Miguel Lago write in *The New York Times*, "In the same way that the antisemites of the past accused the omnipotent, maleficent Jews of being guilty of crimes of all kinds . . . for Mr. Zemmour there is no crime for which Muslims are not guilty."[134] Meanwhile, the left now argued that universalism was forced assimilation, "erasing difference in favour of conservative cultural norms"[135] and was inadequate for the purpose of fighting inequality. In February 2021, the Macron government announced "an investigation into academic research that feeds 'Islamo-leftist' tendencies that 'corrupt society.'"[136] The government expressed concern about studies of race, gender and particularly post-colonial and intersectional studies. Meanwhile the French Parliament was considering a draft law against Islamism, the belief that Islam should guide social and political as well as personal life, a draft law proposed by President Macron.

133 Note 50, p. 144.
134 "France's Old Bigotry Finds a New Face," *The New York Times*, December 2, 2021 https://www.nytimes.com/2021/12/02/opinion/eric-zemmour-france-jews. html?referringSource=articleShare (accessed December 2, 2021).
135 Natasha Lehrer, "France's Model Minority," in Jo Glanville (ed.), *Looking for an Enemy* (London: Short Books, 2021), p. 50.
136 See Norimitsu Onishi and Constant Méheut, "Heating Up Culture Wars, France to Scour Universities for Ideas That 'Corrupt Society,'" *The New York Times*, February 18, 2021 https://www.nytimes.com/2021/02/18/world/europe/france-universities-culture-wars. html (accessed February 19, 2021). The expression "Islamo-leftism" was coined in the early 2000s by the French historian Pierre-André Taguieff to describe a political alliance between Islamist radicals and far-left militants against the United States and Israel.

BRITAIN

There are about 300,000 Jews in the United Kingdom, half of 1 per cent of the country's population. Almost all live in England, most in North London.[137] The core of the population are descendants of about 200,000 Jews who arrived on British shores between 1880 and 1919. Most of these were Russian refugees fleeing pogroms. My grandparents, Volodya and Manya Slavouski, were among them, arriving in 1914 via Berlin and Paris. They went to live in North London.

British Jews are the most likely of any European Jews to say that religion is the main factor in defining their Jewish identity (over 60 per cent).[138] It is not clear why this is the case. Most British Jews are also committed to Zionism. This dual commitment is a paradox, since Zionism is often considered by British Jews as "a secular, ethnic alternative to a synagogue-based Jewish identity." Zionism is frequently regarded as a way of being Jewish that is "neither time-consuming nor socially burdensome."[139] But it seems likely that advocating Zionism will become—if it hasn't already—socially and politically burdensome, as controversy over Zionism increases, something that is well underway in Britain.

Strong commitment to both Judaism and Zionism makes British Jews more militant about perceived antisemitism than many Jewish communities elsewhere in the world. The case of Jeremy Corbyn is an example of this militancy. Corbyn was leader of the opposition Labour Party from 2015 to 2020 and therefore a potential U.K. prime minister. A strong supporter of Palestinian rights, he was consequently seen by many as an antisemite.[140] It was widely reported early in 2019 that a

---

137 See Institute for Jewish Policy Research, *Key Trends in the British Jewish Community* (London: 2011), p. 11. https://www.jpr.org.uk/documents/Key%20trends%20 in%20the%20British%20Jewish%20community.pdf (accessed December 26, 2020).
138 See Sergio DellaPergola and L. Daniel Staetsky, note 9, p. 9.
139 Todd Endelman, *The Jews of Britain 1656 to 2000* (Berkeley: University of California Press, 2002), p. 238.
140 For a good summary of Corbyn's missteps, see Sam Knight, "Jeremy Corbyn's Anti-Semitism Crisis, *The New Yorker*, August 12, 2018 https://www.newyorker.

third or more of British Jews were so alarmed at the prospect of Corbyn becoming prime minister in the election scheduled for later that year that they were considering moving to another country. Ironically, a few years earlier the BBC reported that French Jews, afraid of antisemitism in their own country, were moving to London in increasing numbers.[141]

The response of officialdom to fear of Corbyn was predictable— a plethora of studies and reports. In early 2016 the Labour Party conducted an inquiry into antisemitism and other forms of racism within the Party, chaired by human rights lawyer Shami Chakrabarti. The Chakrabarti Report of June 2016 found that the Labour Party was "not overrun" by antisemitism, Islamophobia, or other forms of racism, but that, "as with wider society," there is evidence of "minority hateful or ignorant attitudes and behaviours festering within a sometimes bitter incivility of discourse."[142] Not to be outdone, in April 2016 the U.K. House of Commons Home Affairs Committee began its own inquiry into antisemitism. The Committee's October 2016 Report noted a 29 per cent increase in police-recorded antisemitic hate crimes in England and some parts of Wales between 2010 and 2015, compared with a 9 per cent increase across all hate crime categories.[143] The Committee examined the festering allegations against Jeremy Corbyn. Its report concluded, "we are not persuaded that he fully appreciates the distinct nature of post-Second World War antisemitism . . . we believe that his lack of consistent leadership on this issue, and his reluctance to separate antisemitism from other forms of racism, has created what some

com/news/letter-from-the-uk/jeremy-corbyns-anti-semitism-crisis (accessed December 29, 2020). Julia Neuberger has pointed out that there is also a history of antisemitism in the Conservative Party. See Neuberger, *Antisemitism* (London: Weidenfeld & Nicolson, 2019), pp. 99–104.

141 Greg Dawson, "Why French Jewish People Are Moving to London," BBC News, February 1, 2016 https://www.bbc.com/news/uk-35430189 (accessed December 27, 2020).

142 *Report of the Shami Chakrabarti Inquiry*, June 30, 2016.

143 See *Antisemitism in the UK* (London: House of Commons, 2016) https://publications.parliament.uk/pa/cm201617/cmselect/cmhaff/136/136.pdf (accessed December 27, 2020) pp. 3–4.

have referred to as a 'safe space' for those with vile attitudes towards Jewish people."[144] But the report cautioned: "It is not antisemitic to criticise the Government of Israel, without additional evidence to suggest antisemitic intent. It is not antisemitic to hold the Israeli Government to the same standards as other liberal democracies, or to take a particular interest in the Israeli Government's policies or actions, without additional evidence to suggest antisemitic intent."[145] As for Zionism, the Report noted that definition of the term was imprecise, but said "'Zionism' as a concept remains a valid topic for academic and political debate, both within and outside Israel." But then, in contradiction, the report said that "the word 'Zionist' (or worse, 'Zio') as a term of abuse, however, has no place in a civilised society. It has been tarnished by its repeated use in antisemitic and aggressive contexts. Antisemites frequently use the word 'Zionist' when they are in fact referring to Jews, whether in Israel or elsewhere."[146] In October 2020 yet another report into antisemitism in the Labour Party was published, this one by the Equality and Human Rights Commission (EHRC), a government body. The report found evidence of political interference into complaints of antisemitism, failure to provide training to handle complaints of antisemitism, illegal harassment, and a failure of party leadership. Corbyn, who criticized the EHRC report, was temporarily suspended from the Party (his membership was restored a month later, but he was not allowed to rejoin the Labour Party caucus in the House of Commons).[147]

Another British institutional expression of "anti-Zionism" causing much commotion in the British Jewish community has been an academic boycott of Israel universities, part of an international

---

144 Note 143, p. 44.
145 Note 143, p. 12.
146 Note 143, p. 15.
147 Two books for those who enjoy inside baseball: Jewish Voice for Labour, *How the EHRC Got It So Wrong: Antisemitism and the Labour Party* (London: Verso, 2021), and David Renton, *Labour's Antisemitism Crisis: What the Left Got Wrong and How to Learn from It* (London: Routledge, 2021).

movement, founded in 2005 known as BDS (for Boycott, Divestment, Sanctions).[148] The seeds of this academic boycott were planted in 2002, when an open letter to *The Guardian* newspaper, ultimately signed by several hundred academics, called for a moratorium on cultural and research links with Israel. This led to controversy and acrimony in British academic institutions which continues to this day. In October 2015, in a highly publicized incident, more than 300 British academics pledged to boycott Israeli academic institutions in protest at "intolerable human rights violations against the Palestinian people."[149] This followed a pledge in February 2015 by several hundred artists and musicians to initiate a cultural boycott of Israel. In 2017 the BBC reported that 17 British students' unions had passed motions to endorse the BDS boycott of Israel.

A 2019 survey found that almost half of British Jews avoid showing visible signs of their Judaism in public because of antisemitism. The survey suggested a "deeply troubling normalisation of antisemitism," with 45 per cent of British adults having some antisemitic views. But another survey taken at the same time suggested that British Jews were more optimistic about their future in the United Kingdom since the end of Jeremy Corbyn's leadership of the Labour Party.[150]

---

148 See the BDS website "Academic Boycott" https://bdsmovement.net/academic-boycott (accessed January 1, 2021). BDS has had little success outside academia. It has three goals: end Israeli occupation of the West Bank and Gaza, give Palestinian refugees a "right of return," and ensure equal rights for Palestinian citizens of Israel.

149 See Peter Walker and Ian Black, "UK Academics Boycott Universities in Israel to Fight for Palestinians' Rights," *The Guardian*, October 27, 2015 https://www.theguardian.com/world/2015/oct/27/uk-academics-boycott-universities-in-israel-to-fight-for-palestinians-rights (accessed December 31, 2020).

150 See Harriet Sherwood, "Half of British Jews Will Not Display Public Sign of Judaism," *The Guardian*, January 17, 2021 https://www.theguardian.com/news/2021/jan/17/half-of-british-jews-will-not-display-public-sign-of-judaism (accessed January 17, 2021).

GERMANY

On a visit to Berlin, I went to a Jewish delicatessen called Mogg for lunch. Mogg is on Auguststrasse in a building that was once a school for Jewish girls. There is a stolperstein in front. A stolperstein ("stumbling stone") is a small concrete and brass plaque bearing the name of a victim of Nazi persecution, set in the pavement in front of the last place the victim lived. You can find them throughout Berlin and in other European cities (there are about 7,000 in Berlin and 70,000 in all of Europe). The stolperstein outside Mogg reads: "Käthe Simonsohn, born 1891, deported 11 July 1942, murdered in Auschwitz."

When Adolf Hitler became German Chancellor in January 1933, there were about 522,000 Jews living in Germany. The Nazis introduced antisemitic laws and rules almost immediately. Many Jews quickly fled. Jewish emigration was possible, although increasingly difficult, until 1941. By 1939 there were only 214,000 Jews left in Germany. In 1945, about 15,000 (the "survivor community") remained. The rest, along with millions of other European Jews, had been murdered. Today there are about 275,000 Jews in Germany, a country of 85 million (some estimates of the number of Jews living in Germany today put the number at considerably less). Most are recent Russian-speaking immigrants from the former republics of the Soviet Union—more of these went to Germany than to Israel—although there are some immigrants from Israel (estimated to be about 20,000) and from the United States (10,000).

Judging by official rhetoric, Germany seems at peace with its Jewish population and welcomes Jews who move from elsewhere. In 2017 the German government adopted the International Holocaust Remembrance Alliance working definition of antisemitism, ignoring the evident flaws in that definition. In May 2019 the German Parliament passed an advisory declaration calling on states and municipalities to deny public funding to any institution that actively supports the BDS movement against Israel (widely but incorrectly regarded in Germany as antisemitic) or questions the right of Israel to exist. In a classic free speech riposte to this declaration, the directors of 32 German cultural institutions released an open letter which said, "instead of curbing anti-Semitism, the resolution has stifled the open exchange of ideas in the public sphere and freedom of expression in the arts, both of which are guaranteed by Germany's constitution."[151] Tension between German politicians and creative artists over this issue has grown since. In the summer of 2022, artwork was removed from display at Documenta, an internationally important art show held every five years in Kassel, Germany, on the grounds that it contained antisemitic caricatures, and the event's director resigned. Allegations were made that those who curated the show were BDS supporters. The Documenta controversy was heated and protracted.[152]

In May 2019, the BBC reported about Germany: "Official figures showed 1,646 hate crimes against Jews were committed in 2018—an increase of 10% on the previous year. Physical attacks against Jews in Germany also rose in the same period, with 62 violent incidents recorded, up from 37 in 2017."[153] Reports had it that the number of hate crimes against Jews increased again, by 13 per cent, in 2019. In October 2019 an attack on a synagogue in Halle on Yom Kippur killed two people. Speaking in September 2020, echoing President Macron's statement the year before about antisemitism in France, Chancellor Angela Merkel said, "many German Jews still do not feel safe and that anti-Semitism in Germany 'never disappeared.'"[154] In 2020 Germany

151 See Melissa Eddy, "German Cultural Leaders Warn Against Ban on Israel Sanctions Movement" *The New York Times*, December 11, 2020 https://www.nytimes.com/2020/12/11/arts/germany-bds-open-letter.html (accessed January 4, 2021).

152 See Alex Marshall, "Furor Over Documenta Highlights a Widening Chasm in Germany," *The New York Times*, August 6, 2022 https://www.nytimes.com/2022/08/06/arts/design/documenta-antisemitism.html (accessed August 20, 2022).

153 "German Jews Warned Not to Wear Kippas After Rise in Anti-Semitism," BBC News, May 26, 2019 https://www.bbc.com/news/world-europe-48411735 (accessed January 2, 2021).

154 "German Chancellor Angela Merkel: 'Many Jews Do Not Feel Safe in Our Country,'" *dw*, September 15, 2020 https://www.dw.com/en/german-chancellor-angela-merkel-many-jews-do-not-feel-safe-in-our-country/a-54931625 (accessed January 2, 2021).

pledged $26 million dollars to fund the security needs of its Jewish minority. In February 2021 the German government released figures on the number of registered antisemitic hate crimes in 2020, showing a continuing upward trend. The ideological motivation of many of these hate crimes is unclear; some are attributed to right-wing extremists; some, to Muslim antisemitism. A study published in 2022 argued that antisemitism is deeply rooted in mainstream German society.[155] In June 2022 the German government reported a 29 per cent increase in antisemitic crimes in 2021 over the previous year (3,027 incidents), most related to right-wing extremism, and mostly comprised of illegal statements and publications (hate speech and Holocaust denial).[156]

It's not just physical security that is at stake. James Angelos has written in *The New York Times* that, in the decades following World War II, "a desire among many Germans to deflect or repress guilt for the Holocaust led to a new form of antipathy toward Jews — a phenomenon that came to be known as 'secondary anti-Semitism,' in which Germans resent Jews for reminding them of their guilt, reversing the victim and perpetrator roles."[157]

SOUTH AFRICA

In the early 2000s my wife and I lived in Cape Town. I was teaching in the law faculty at the University of Cape Town. We became friends

155 American Jewish Committee, *Antisemitismus in Deutschland* https://ajcgermany. org/system/files/document/AJC-Berlin_Antisemitismus%20in%20Deutschland_ Eine%20Repräsentativbefragung.pdf. And see Deutsche Welle, "Antisemitism 'Deeply Rooted' in German Society," https://www.dw.com/en/antisemitism-deeply-rooted-in-german-society/a-61750177 (accessed May 12, 2022).

156 See Toby Axelrod, "Germany Records 29% Increase in Antisemitic Crimes in 2021," *The Times of Israel*, June 10, 2022 https://www.timesofisrael.com/german-government-reports-29-increase-in-antisemitic-crimes-in-2021/ (accessed June 19, 2022).

157 James Angelos, "The New German Anti-Semitism," *The New York Times Magazine*, May 21, 2019 https://www.nytimes.com/2019/05/21/magazine/anti-semitism-germany.html (accessed September 23, 2021).

with David and Ann Susman, members of the South African Jewish community. David Susman had been Managing Director of Woolworth, a large South African retail chain. His father, Elie Susman, had been a founder of the company. Elie and his brother Harry had left Lithuania at the turn of the last century and went first to what is now Zambia (then Northern Rhodesia), crossing the Zambezi River and settling in the small town of Livingstone on the River's banks, close by Victoria Falls, where they became cattle ranchers, emerged as leaders of the tiny local Jewish community, and built a synagogue. In the 1930s they became partners in Woolworth, then a fledgling business. In 1948 David Susman volunteered as a fighter pilot in the new Israeli air force at war with Arab forces. The Susman family story was a saga of Jewish generations in Africa, wandering, striving, and succeeding—leaving Lithuania, crossing the Zambezi, cattle ranching in Northern Rhodesia, founding a synagogue in a small African town, fighter pilot in Israel, eventually achieving wealth and prominence. Ironically, Jews who fled Europe for Africa because of antisemitism later found themselves once again the object of prejudice, this time not because of their race but because of their skin colour.

There are about 52,000 Jews in South Africa, down from about 120,000 in 1970 and 62,000 in 2001. It remains the largest Jewish community in Africa by far, but is less than one tenth of 1 per cent of South Africa's overall population. Most South African Jews, like the Susmans, are descendants of those who left the Grand Duchy of Lithuania to escape persecution, starting at the end of the 19th century (the Grand Duchy comprised present-day Lithuania and parts of Belarus, Ukraine, Latvia, and Poland.)[158]

Many Jews left South Africa during the apartheid years. Numbers continue to dwindle as emigration—driven by economic uncertainty, fear of political and racial instability, and a high crime rate—increases. Most South African Jews who emigrate go to Israel. A number of those

---

158 See Karina Simonson, "Litvaks in South Africa: How to Photograph Nelson Mandela?" *Ufahamu: A Journal of African Studies, 38(1)* 2014 https://escholarship. org/content/qt0fw830ps/qt0fw830ps.pdf (accessed January 8, 2021).

remaining contemplate doing so. Other destinations are Britain, the United States, Australia, and Canada. Those who remain in South Africa form a strong and vibrant community, religiously observant, not likely to assimilate, with a relatively small rate of intermarriage (only 19 per cent of South African Jews marrying between 2015 and 2019 married a non-Jew). The Jewish identity is particularly strong. It is reported, "81% attend a Passover *seder* meal and 76% fast on Yom Kippur every year. 21% refrain from using electric light switches on Shabbat every week."[159] There is strong, but qualified, support for Israel. According to one survey, 83 per cent of South African Jews "feel it is never acceptable for Jews to publicly support a boycott of Israel"[160] and 69 per cent define themselves as Zionists.[161] But the treatment of Palestinians is a subject of high controversy, among both Jews and non-Jews. When I lived in Cape Town, I was struck by the extent of opposition in the Jewish community to Israel's Palestinian policies. The fact that Israel once supplied weapons and training to the apartheid government of South Africa had not been forgotten.[162] The revered Desmond Tutu, one-time Anglican Archbishop of Cape Town, close ally of Nelson Mandela, and someone who struggled against apartheid and racism his whole life, was a strong critic of Israel's Palestinian policies, as was Mandela himself.

In general, there are few antisemitic incidents in South Africa, certainly compared to European countries, but sensitivities remain. The 2019 Graham study reported: "92% feel that anti-Israel sentiment has increased over the past five years; 74% feel the same about anti-Jewish sentiment."[163]

---

159 See David Graham, note 11.
160 Graham, note 11, p. 8.
161 Graham, note 11, p. 56.
162 See Judy Maltz, "Jews Are Leaving South Africa Once Again — but Don't Blame BDS," *Haaretz*, June 16, 2019 https://www.haaretz.com/world-news/asia-and-australia/.premium-jews-are-leaving-south-africa-once-again-but-don-t-blame-bds-1.7366376 (accessed January 8, 2021).
163 Graham, note 11, p. 10.

CANADA

There are about 400,000 Jews in Canada,[164] slightly more than 1 per cent of the country's population. About 250,000 of them live in Toronto and Montreal. The Canadian Jewish community is the fourth largest Jewish community in the world, and may soon overtake France to become the third largest. A 2018 Environics Survey reported that the Canadian community is cohesive, with a rising but still low rate of intermarriage; grows slowly; is not religiously observant to any great degree; and has an emotional attachment to the State of Israel.[165]

There was considerable antisemitism in Canada until well into the 20th century. A wartime federal government anti-Jewish immigration policy was summed up by the notorious phrase "none is too many"[166] attributed to Frederick Blair, the Canadian director of immigration between 1936 and 1943. In 1939 the German ocean liner MS St. Louis with 908 Jewish refugees on board was turned away from Canada with the agreement of Prime Minister Mackenzie King. The ship returned to Europe. Many of those on board died in concentration camps. After the war, Canada's immigration policy changed. In the late 1940s, about 40,000 Holocaust survivors were admitted. Later, a significant number of Jews emigrated to Canada from the former Soviet Union, the United States, North African countries, South Africa, France, and Israel. My own immediate family came from the United Kingdom in 1954. About 30 per cent of Jews in Canada are immigrants.[167]

---

164 "For most Canadian Jews today, the basis of Jewish identity is less about religion than about culture, ethnicity, or a combination of culture, ethnicity, and religion." See Robert Brym, Keith Neuman and Rhonda Lenton, *2018 Survey of Jews in Canada* (Toronto: Environics Institute for Survey Research, 2018), p. 5. https://www.environicsinstitute. org/docs/default-source/project-documents/2018-survey-of-jews-in-canada/2018-survey-of-jews-in-canada---final-report.pdf?sfvrsn=2994ef6_2 (accessed January 15, 2021).

165 Note 164.

166 Also the title of a well-known book by Irving Abella and Harold Troper (Toronto: Lester & Orpen Dennys, 1983).

167 Environics Institute, note 164, p. 12.

In March 1945, Toronto Rabbi Abraham Feinberg, a prominent Canadian Jewish leader of the time, described Canadian antisemitism in a *Maclean's* article.[168]

> Jews are kept out of most ski clubs. Sundry summer colonies (even on municipally owned land), fraternities, and at least one Rotary Club operate under written or unwritten "Gentiles Only" signs. Many bank positions are not open to Jews. Only three Jewish male physicians have been admitted to non-Jewish Hospital staffs in Toronto. McGill University has instituted a rule requiring in effect at least a 10% higher academic average for Jewish applicants; in certain schools of the University of Toronto anti-Jewish bias is being felt. City Councils debate whether Jewish petitioners should be permitted to build a synagogue; property deeds in some areas bar resale to them. I have seen crude handbills circulated thanking Hitler for his massacre of 80,000 Jews in Kiev.
>
> . . .
>
> Even the friendliest Gentiles . . . tend to regard the Jew as a "problem." This was affirmed in so many words by 1,125 students at the University of Manitoba. In their answers to a recent questionnaire a majority listed the Jewish problem as second in importance (following the French Canadian and preceding the Japanese).

Growing up in Winnipeg in the 1950s and 1960s, I had little awareness of all this. As a young man I went to the University of Manitoba, where Jews had once been a "problem," although in the 1960s, when I was a student there, I felt no trace of this attitude. My family rented a cottage at Victoria Beach on Lake Winnipeg for a couple of summers. When people who knew us found this out, they were surprised. Jews weren't

---

168 "'Those Jews'. We fight Hitler's creed overseas . . . but we have a seedling of it right here at home, says this Rabbi," *Maclean's*, March 1, 1945 https://archive.macleans.ca/article/1945/3/1/those-jews (accessed January 13, 2021).

supposed to go to Victoria Beach. It was understood. In 1943, John Dafoe, editor of the Winnipeg Free Press, wrote: "The Nazis of Europe are making it plain to the Jewish people that they would not live with them. Here, in Manitoba, the summer residents of Victoria Beach are engaged in a similar crusade."[169]

The 2018 Environics Survey reported that one-third of Canadian Jews believe Jews in Canada "often" experience discrimination. Fifty per cent say this happens "sometimes." Canadian Jews believe that discrimination is more often experienced by Indigenous people, Muslims, and Black people, and to a lesser extent gays and lesbians.[170] "Negative experiences" of Jews include being called offensive names, being snubbed in social settings, and being criticized for defending or criticizing policies or actions of the State of Israel. It was reported by B'nai Brith that in 2020 antisemitic acts in Canada went up by almost 20 per cent. "Some 44% of the violent incidents last year were COVID-related, half of those against visibly observant Jews who were denied service at various retailers, spat on, assaulted randomly, pelted by items, and shot with air pellets . . ."[171]

169 See Chloé Dioré de Périgny, "'Unwanted People': When Manitoba's Beaches Were Forbidden to Jews," CBC News, February 2, 2020 https://www.cbc.ca/news/canada/manitoba/when-manitoba-s-beaches-were-forbidden-to-jews-1.5448883 (accessed January 16, 2021). The literature on the Jews of Manitoba is particularly rich. See Arthur A. Chiel, *The Jews in Manitoba* (Toronto: University of Toronto Press, 1961), and Allan Levine, *Coming of Age: A History of the Jewish People of Manitoba* (Winnipeg: Heartland, 2009). Chiel describes "the splits and breaches" in the religious life of the early Winnipeg Jewish community arising out of conflict between Eastern European traditionalists and western European liberals (pp. 90–91). Levine describes arguments that roiled the Manitoba Jewish community. He comments: "The one issue upon which Manitoba Jews formed a united front was in combatting prejudice and discrimination . . . It is the great irony of Jewish history that anti-Semitism, though by no means the only factor, has played a major role in Jewish survival." (p. 22) Levine describes in detail the prejudice and discrimination endured at times by Manitoba Jews.

170 Note 164, p. 47.

171 Sue-Ann Levy, "Anti-Semitic Acts Jump 18.6% in 2020, Says B'nai Brith Report," *Toronto Sun*, April 26, 2021 https://torontosun.com/news/national/anti-semitic-acts-jump-18-6-in-2020-says-bnai-brith-report (accessed April 27, 2021).

Most of the year I live in an apartment building in downtown Toronto. On the ground floor is a branch of an Israeli expresso and coffee chain. On March 27, 2020, the words "Zionists not welcome" were spray-painted on the side of the building. This inconsequential event was reported by a vigilant Israeli press.[172] More recently a sticker was put on the coffee shop's window—"Boycott Israeli Apartheid. Free Palestine." The Israeli press missed that incident.

CODA: THE GREAT HALL, LVIV, UKRAINE

In September 2017, my wife and I attended the 83rd PEN International Congress in Lviv, Ukraine, as a member of the Canadian PEN delegation. Lviv (also known as Lvov, Lwów, and Lemberg) is a few hundred kilometres from Cherkasy in central Ukraine, the hometown of my family on my father's side, a place my grandfather left more than a hundred years before. Between 1914 and 1944, control of Lviv changed eight times, as the armies of competing powers marched in and out. In the first half of the 20th century, Lviv was at different times part of Austria, Russia, Poland, Germany, the Soviet Union, and, eventually, an independent Ukraine.

The Germans occupied Lviv from 1941 to 1944. Hans Frank was the Nazi governor-general of occupied Poland and the province of Galicia, which included Lviv. On August 1, 1942, he gave a speech in the Great Hall of Lviv University. He announced plans for the Jews who lived in the nearby ghetto—*Die gross Aktion*. A week later the roundup of these Jews and their transport to the death camp of Belzec, fifty miles to the northeast, began. In 1941, the Jewish population of Lviv was more than 200,000, about 50 per cent of the city's total population. By 1944, none were left. The city was *Judenfrei*.

---

172 "Spate of Anti-Semitic Graffiti Hits Toronto," *Arutzsheva*, April 14, 2020 https:// www.israelnationalnews.com/News/News.aspx/278675 (accessed January 27, 2021).

Seventy-five years after Frank's announcement of *Die gross Aktion* in the Great Hall of Lviv University, British human rights lawyer Philippe Sands delivered the keynote address to the PEN Congress in the very same room, from the very same lectern.[173] My wife and I sat in the second row. A photograph exists of Frank delivering his 1942 speech.[174] Sitting in the second row for Frank's speech, in the seats my wife and I occupied for Sands' address, were two men in Nazi uniforms.[175] "This place," said my wife, "is a crime scene."

Lviv had been a crime scene before, many times. In November 1918 victorious Polish soldiers, joined by townspeople, conducted a brutal pogrom in Lviv that lasted three days. Jeffrey Veidlinger writes that some 100 murdered Jews "were deliberately slaughtered by organized soldiers, who were encouraged by a supportive population that included not only antisemitic ruffians but also members of high society . . ."[176] This and other pogroms, in what is now Ukraine, following World War I, argues Veidlinger, who describes many of the pogroms in great detail, helped lay the groundwork for the Holocaust.[177] They "established a precedent that could be built on in the future . . . Most important, the value of Jewish life had been debased."[178]

173 See https://pen-international.org/es/print/4602 (accessed April 12, 2021).

174 See Philippe Sands, *East West Street* (New York: Alfred A. Knopf, 2016), pp. 232–7, for an account of all this. The picture of Frank in the Great Hall is on p. 235. Sands' grandfather was born in Lviv. See also Sands, *The Ratline* (New York: Alfred A. Knopf, 2021).

175 For a horrifying account of the antisemitic history of Lviv, see Aly, note 32, pp. 106–14.

176 Veidlinger, note 76, p. 87.

177 Veidlinger writes that between November 1918 and March 1921 over one thousand pogroms took place in Ukraine, and that forty thousand Jews were directly killed and another seventy thousand subsequently perished as a direct result of the attacks. Note 76, pp. 4–5.

178 Note 76, p. 374.

CHAPTER 3

JEWS AND MUSLIMS

IS RECONCILIATION POSSIBLE?

Are Muslims antisemitic? Are Jews Islamophobic? Can Jews and Muslims reconcile in the modern age of identity politics? Today Jews and Muslims seem at daggers drawn. But it wasn't always like that, and need not be in the years to come.

Judaism and Islam are two of the world's three great monotheistic religions. Both regard the Prophet Abraham as a founder. Both believe in a Divine Law revealed by God. Jerusalem is a holy city for both. They share a similar conception of law; Islam's legal tradition, Sharia, is modelled on the Jewish legal tradition, Halakha.[179] There is similarity in their religious practices, such as fixed hours for prayer, requirements for ritual purification, particular geographic orientation prior to prayer,

---

179 See Meir M. Bar-Asher, *Jews and the Qur'an* (Princeton: Princeton University Press, 2021), p. xi (Foreword by Mustafa Akyol). Bar-Asher analyzes the "ambivalence" of the Qur'an towards Judaism.

dietary laws, and the fixing of the calendar.[180] Each has influenced the literature and art of the other.[181] Some non-Muslims have even argued that Islam was substantially influenced by Jewish theology, but Muslims repudiate this idea: God, they insist, by his very nature, cannot be influenced. Likewise, when it came to the Prophet Mohammed (571–632 CE), the founder of Islam, medieval Jews had difficulty believing that God would send a Prophet who was not a Jew.[182]

David Nirenberg argues that the early community of Believers, as Muslims were originally called, "sought to appropriate the prophetic traditions of Judaism while at the same time distancing itself from them."[183] Judaism had a complicated utility for Islam: "[T]he Jewish ambivalences produced in the prophetic generation came to serve as paradigm or pattern of thought for the Islamic community as it expanded with almost unimaginable rapidity . . . The simultaneous inclusion and exclusion of Judaism became for Islam . . . a structuring principle of the world, one through which Islamic truth was explored, discovered, and articulated."[184] For the Prophet, theological differences between his followers and Christians and Jews were not important. Maxime Rodinson writes, in his superb biography of Mohammed, "He was convinced, not unreasonably, that the Voice which spoke to him was repeating essentially the same message as that which had been given to the 'Peoples of the Book' and which was common to them all. The rest was mere detail."[185]

Despite theological kinship, in the early days Jews were seen as strange and a nuisance by Muslims, and this sense of their difference only grew. Rodinson writes that in Mecca "people suffered from their commercial competition and feared the potential power of such busy

---

180 See Bar-Asher, note 179, ch. IV.
181 See Bernard Lewis, note 92, pp. 79–81.
182 See Martin Lings, *Muhammad: His Life Based on the Earliest Sources* (Rochester: Inner Tradition, 1983), p. 129.
183 Note 14, p. 164.
184 Note 14, p. 165.
185 Note 26, p. 133.

and energetic bodies, and . . . wondered at their curious habits, such as their reluctance to eat such foods as camel-hump lard, which everyone else liked, and mocked their clumsy Arabic, full of words culled from Hebrew or Aramaic . . ."[186] In his book *In Ishmael's House*, the historian Martin Gilbert captures the ambiguity of Jewish/Muslim history. Following the death of the Prophet, writes Gilbert, "Muslims had to decide in their relations with the Jews whether to see them as a cursed people or as a people protected by Islam. Mohammed's example gave them ample reason to take either view. Although he had protected Jews living under *dhimmi* status and granted them religious freedom, he had also subjugated them and punished them severely . . . In the fourteen centuries since Mohammed's death, Jews in Muslim lands have faced both cursing and protection."[187]

For long periods of history, Jews fared worse at the hands of Christians than at the hands of Muslims. Indeed, Muslims often offered Jews protection from Christians. At the end of the 15th century, following a period of severe persecution and forced conversion to Christianity, more than 100,000 Jews were expelled from Spain and Portugal. Many of these refugees found security, admittedly not always reliable, in the lands of the Ottoman Empire. Bernard Lewis observes, "For centuries Jews in great numbers continued to travel from various parts of Christian Europe into the Ottoman lands, attracted by the reports they had heard about the greater tolerance and greater opportunity offered by the Ottoman government."[188] Or, as Lewis puts it elsewhere, Jews under Islamic rule "were never free from discrimination, but only rarely subject to persecution . . . their situation was never as bad

---

186 Note 26, p. 133.
187 Martin Gilbert, note 89, p. 26. The complex rules for the *dhimmi* ("protected people") status, codified by the eighth Umayyad Caliph, Abd Al-Azziz, who reigned from 717 to 720, in the so-called "Pact of Umar," resulted in the subjugation of Jews to Muslims, although Jews were guaranteed basic privileges. The *Dhimmi* rules prevailed in the Ottoman empire until the end of the 19th century. Christian and Zoroastrians also had *dhimmi* status. The *dhimmis* were required to pay tribute in perpetuity (the *umma*) to the Muslim community.
188 Note 92, p. 121.

as in Christendom at its worst, nor ever as good as in Christendom at its best."[189]

Lewis distinguishes between Islamic and Christian types of antisemitism in the Middle Ages. This is a distinction that reverberates in modern times. He writes, "In Islamic society hostility to the Jew is non-theological. It is not related to any specific Islamic doctrine, nor to any specific circumstance in Islamic sacred history. For Muslims, it is not part of the birth pangs of their religion, as it is for Christians. It is rather the usual attitude of the dominant to the subordinate, of the majority to the minority, without that additional theological and therefore psychological dimension that gives Christian anti-Semitism its unique and special character."[190] Islamic antisemitism is less deep-rooted than Christian antisemitism, less virulent, more dependent on circumstances, and more amenable to change.

During the Middle Ages most Jews lived in Muslim countries. Lewis writes, "whatever was creative and significant in Jewish life happened in Islamic lands. The Jewish communities of Europe formed a kind of cultural dependency on the Jews of the far more advanced and sophisticated Islamic world, extending from Muslim Spain in the west to Iraq, Iran, and Central Asia in the east."[191] The Jews adopted Arabic as their language, producing a Judaeo-Islamic culture, "an assimilation to Islamic modes of thought and patterns of behaviour . . ."[192] Lewis says of this period, "Jews and Muslims had extensive and intimate contacts that involved social as well as intellectual association—cooperation, commingling, even personal friendship."[193] In the late Middle Ages, this began to change, and the centre of Jewish gravity shifted from the Islamic world to Europe. In the modern era, as we have seen, it has shifted from Europe to the United States and Israel. The loss of

189 Note 25, p. 121.
190 Note 92, p. 85.
191 Note 92, p. 67.
192 Note 92, p. 78.
193 Note 92, p. 88.

extensive and intimate contacts and personal friendships between Jews and Muslims makes possible mindless mutual antipathy based on stereotypes.

In recent years there has been a rarified dispute over how much mutual sympathy between Jews and Muslims really existed over the centuries. Giselle Littman (who writes under the name Bat-Ye'or) is a leading, but controversial and much-criticized, exponent of "a gloomy representation of Jewish life in the lands of Islam that emphasizes the continuity of oppression and persecution from the time of Muhammad until the demise of most Arab Jewish communities in the aftermath of the 1948 Arab-Israeli war."[194] Ye'or describes in detail what she construes as the subordination, even degradation, through the centuries, of the *Dhimmi* in Arab lands.[195] Some have suggested that expression of this view has a contemporary political purpose, that it is intended to justify harsh treatment of Palestinians by Israel and in particular the rejection of Palestinian claims of dispossession. Ye'or emphasizes modern declarations by Islamic leaders of the need for *jihad* (war) against Israel on behalf of Palestinian Arabs. Lyn Julius, daughter of Iraqi Jews, has written at great length, and passionately, about the persecution of Jews in Arab lands, leading most of them to become "refugees" and flee to Israel in the late 1940s.[196]

Meanwhile, the relationship between Jews and Muslims has been badly damaged by the never-ending Palestine conflict and various wars, particularly the Arab–Israel War of Independence in 1948, the Six-Day War of 1967 when Israel defeated the armies of Egypt, Syria, and Jordan, captured substantial territories, and acquired a new

194 Joel Beinin, *The Dispersion of Egyptian Jewry: Culture, Politics, and the Formation of a Modern Diaspora* (Berkeley: University of California Press, 1998). http://ark. cdlib.org/ark:/13030/ft2290045n/ https://publishing.cdlib.org/ucpressebooks/ view?docId=ft2290045n;chunk.id=ch1;doc.view=print (accessed May 15, 2021).

195 See Bat Ye'or, *The Dhimmi: Jews and Christian Under Islam* (Cranbury: Associated University Presses, 1985). See also Lyn Julius, "When Will the 'Happy Dhimmi' Myth Be Discredited?" *Jewish News Syndicate*, September 23, 2021 https://www. jns.org/opinion/when-will-the-happy-dhimmi-myth-be-discredited/ (accessed September 24, 2021).

196 Note 92.

subject Arab population of over a million, and the Israeli invasion of Lebanon in 1982. Many commentators have argued that the dispute over Palestine is primarily geo-political, mostly about territory and dispossession, and not religious, ethnic, or cultural. Bernard Lewis has written: "The Arab-Israeli conflict is in its essence a political one—a clash between peoples and states over real issues, not a matter of prejudice and persecution."[197] Even seeking the destruction of Israel is not necessarily antisemitic at its core. Lewis argues, "In the view of most Arabs, the creation of the State of Israel was an act of injustice, and its continued existence a standing aggression. To those who hold this view, the correction of that injustice and the removal of that aggression are legitimate political objectives."[198] Others, such as Julia Neuberger, a London rabbi and member of the U.K. House of Lords, profoundly disagree. Neuberger writes, "Explicit antisemitism is now commonplace in Middle Eastern political discourse. And much of it is being reimported into Europe, where it started, and, sadly, it can now be found among some impoverished and disaffected Muslim immigrant communities."[199] Neuberger concedes, however, that a significant number of Muslims reject antisemitism, and, indeed, stand in solidarity with Jews when they are attacked. President Kais Saied of Tunisia has said, "The Jews are not the problem . . . We work with Jews and we will protect Jews. But not those who have Israeli passports. Never."[200] Meanwhile the Abraham Accords of the 2020s, so named to emphasize the shared origins and beliefs of Judaism and Islam, have committed (to date) the United Arab Emirates, Sudan, Bahrain, and Morocco to normalizing relations with Israel.

The connection between Islam and Judaism, and their peoples, has been complex and ever-changing. How to divine their modern

---

197 Note 92, p. 237.
198 Note 92, pp. 241–2.
199 Neuberger, note 140, p. 21.
200 Quoted by Eldad Beck, "How Can Tunisia's Jews Escape National Quagmire?" *Israel Hayom*, September 6, 2021 https://www.israelhayom.com/2021/09/06/how-can-tunisias-jews-escape-national-quagmire/ (accessed September 11, 2021).

relationship, the interweaving of friendship and hostility, of peace and conflict? Sometimes the treatment of Jews by Muslims has been good. Sometimes it has been bad. The relationship remains curious and surprising. The 2020 Pew survey of American Jews reported that nearly four-in-ten U.S. Jews feel they have something in common with Muslims. American Jews who do not identify with any particular branch of Judaism are more likely to say they have something in common with Muslims than with Orthodox Jews.[201]

ALMOST ALL GONE NOW

In 1945 the combined Jewish population of Muslim countries was more than a million. Now it is less than ten thousand. Continued, if episodic, oppression of Jews by Muslims, political instability and economic poverty in Muslim countries, and the creation of Israel offering safety and an apparently better life with full citizenship, led to a massive exodus. In the 1940s about 300,000 Jews lived in Morocco; today there are 3,000 or so. Once, Turkey had 250,000 Jews; today it has less than 20,000. In 1948, Egypt had a Jewish population of about 75,000; now the Egyptian Jewish population is estimated to be ten. In the early 1940s, Iraq had about 150,000 Jews; now, there are said to be only four left.[202] In 1948, Yemen had 63,000 Jews; now there are less than 200. In 1948, 20,000 Jews lived in Lebanon; about 100 remain. In 1948, 30,000 Jews lived in Syria; only a handful are left. In 1948, 40,000 Jews lived in Libya; the last Jew in the country, Esmeralda Meghnagi, died in 2002, bringing to an end a community that traced its origins to the 3rd century BCE.[203] In 1948, about 105,000 Jews lived in Tunisia;

201 Pew Research Center, *Jewish Americans in 2020*, May 11, 2021 https://www. pewforum.org/2021/05/11/jewish-americans-in-2020/ (accessed May 12, 2021).

202 See Holly Johnston, "The Last Jewish Doctor of Baghdad," *Rudaw*, March 18, 2021 https://www.rudaw.net/english/middleeast/iraq/18032021 (accessed March 21, 2021).

203 Jewish Virtual Library, *Jews in Islamic Countries: Libya*, https://www.jewishvirtual library.org/jews-of-libya (accessed June 1, 2021).

about 1,500 live there now. In 1948, about 150,000 Jews lived in Algeria; by 2003 approximately forty were left. Afghanistan's only remaining Jew, the controversial and disliked Zebulon Simantov, who looked after the synagogue in Kabul, was said to have left for Israel in 2021 but was apparently still in the country when the Taliban seized control in August 2021 (although it is believed that he has since gone). In much of the modern Arab world an Arab has never met a Jew. His conception of a Jew is based, not on personal day-to-day experience, but on rumour, politically inspired caricatures, and presentations on social media.

MOROCCO

Once Morocco had the largest Jewish community in the Muslim world. Today, almost all the Jews are gone. But Morocco increasingly seeks to recognize and embrace its Jewish past, more aggressively than any other Arab country, suggesting the possibility of worldwide reconciliation and a new mutual respect between Muslims and Jews. Jamaa Baida, the director of Morocco's national archives, has said, "The uprooting of the Jews is akin to a painful sore in Morocco's national history."[204] Morocco's example may be encouraging other Arab states to have a gentler attitude towards Jews. The United Arab Emirates, for example, is attempting to establish new Jewish communities.[205]

In February 2019, I was in Fez in northern inland Morocco. I walked through the streets of the old walled city, through what had been the Jewish quarter and the Jewish cemetery. In the 1940s about 300,000 Jews lived in Morocco. About 25,000 of them lived in Fez, in the Jewish

204 See Ofer Aderet, "Synagogue Ruins Tell Secrets of Jewish Community in Morocco's Atlas Mountains," *Haaretz*, December 27, 2021 https://www.haaretz.com/archaeology/MAGAZINE-israeli-and-moroccan-research-team-discovers-lost-jewish-lives-in-atlas-mountains-1.10494305 (accessed December 28, 2021).
205 See "The Arab World Is Re-embracing Its Jews," *The Economist*, January 22, 2022 https://www.economist.com/middle-east-and-africa/the-arab-world-is-re-embracing-its-jews/21807243 (accessed January 24, 2022).

quarter or *mellāh* founded in 1438 and intended both to isolate and protect Jews.[206] When Morocco became independent in 1956, many Moroccan Jews still considered themselves to be *dhimmi* rather than full citizens. With the creation of Israel in 1948, there was a place to go where they would not have a lesser status. In the 1950s and 1960s most Jews left Morocco for Israel (some went to France and Canada). Today less than a hundred Jews live in Fez. There is one active synagogue. There are about 3,000 Jews in all of Morocco (some estimates put the number as high as 6,000), most of them in Casablanca.

For many years, the Jews in Fez prospered as goldsmiths, lace-makers, embroiderers, tailors, and manufacturers of goldthread. It was not always an easy or safe life. A pogrom in 1465 wiped out most of the residents of the *mellāh*. In 1790 the Sultan of Morocco, Moulay Yazid, expelled Jews from the city (two years later his successor allowed them to return).[207] In 1820 the Udaya, a neighbouring Muslim tribe, plundered the Jewish quarter and abducted Jewish women.[208] In 1834 a seventeen-year-old Jewish woman, Sol Hachuel, was beheaded in the main marketplace of Fez for refusing to convert to Islam.[209] In 1912, Muslims looted and burned the *mellāh* for three days, killing more than sixty Jews and leaving ten thousand homeless (this is known as the *tritl*).[210]

Despite a history sad in many ways, and the fact that few Jews remain there, many Moroccans think of Fez as a Jewish city. The American anthropologist Oran Kosansky has written: "Muslim men and women, especially those old enough to have living memories of

---

206 For a contemporary account of life in the Fez *mellāh* in the early 17th century, see an original document reproduced by Bat Ye'or, note 195, pp. 355–9.

207 For a contemporary account of these events, see Bat Ye'or, note 195, pp. 366–9.

208 For a contemporary account, see Bat Ye'or, note 195, pp. 293–4.

209 This is a legendary incident. See, among many sources, Jewish Encyclopedia https://www.jewishencyclopedia.com/articles/6997-hachuel-sol (accessed June 1, 2021).

210 See, e.g., Lyn Julius, "When the Jews Sheltered with the Sultan's Lions," *Jewish News*, April 16, 2012 https://blogs.timesofisrael.com/when-the-jews-sheltered-with-the-sultans-lions/ (accessed June 1, 2021).

Jewish neighbors, often express nostalgia for those who departed. This nostalgia extends beyond the mellah and its Jewish populace; Fez as a whole is read by Moroccans as a Jewish city. In so reading Fez, Muslims indicate the possibility of a shared identity with their departed Jewish neighbors . . . For Moroccans, losing Jewish neighbours has meant losing a part of oneself."[211]

Feelings like these go beyond Fez, certainly when it comes to older Moroccans. One Arab from the small town of Akka told a visiting anthropologist, Aomar Boum, "When the Jews left Akka, it was like a company of one thousand workers that went bankrupt. Akka is still waiting for its Jews to prosper again."[212] There is a Moroccan saying, still used sometimes, "A market without Jews is like bread without salt." But young Moroccans feel differently. Boum writes that older generational groups "mainly invoke a repertoire of images, discursive tropes, and a lexicon from the traditional worldview when Muslims and Jews were neighbours. On the other hand, the disenfranchised Arab youth rely on a different knowledge, which is largely influenced by a set of imagined ideas of 'Jewishness.' . . . Members of the older cohorts tend to express feelings of friendship and amicable relations toward Jews. By contrast, younger cohorts mostly describe them as evil and threatening to Muslim values and tradition."[213] According to Boum, the reason for the difference is simple. Older Moroccans had intimate knowledge of Jews, or received such knowledge from their parents, grandparents, and great-grandparents. Younger Moroccans have never met a Jew, respond solely to media and notions about the Palestinian–Israeli conflict, and rebel against the social and cultural views of their family. There has been what Boum describes as a "fracturing of memory

211 "Reading Jewish Fez: On the Cultural Identity of a Moroccan City," *The Journal of the International Institute* Volume 8, Issue 3, 2001 https://quod.lib.umich.edu/j/jii/4750978.0008.305/--reading-jewish-fez-on-the-cultural-identity-of-a-moroccan?rgn=main;view=fulltext (accessed March 3, 2021).

212 Aomar Boum, *Memories of Absence: How Muslims Remember Jews in Morocco* (Stanford: Stanford University Press, 2013), p. 34.

213 Boum, note 212, p. 157.

and knowledge transmissions." Personal relationships with neighbours have been replaced by social media posts. In the absence of personal knowledge, it is easy for the mind to be prejudiced, even poisoned. If an Arab has never met a Jew, it is easy for him to succumb to antisemitism, to embrace an imagined idea rather than a real person.

Neta Elkayam, an Israeli singer whose grandparents and parents emigrated from Morocco, went back for a visit with a friend: "We both felt like we were walking on air. This is how our place needs to feel. I felt home. I felt filled with happiness. I felt like a complete stranger at the same time. A lot of people on the streets looked like me or like people I knew from my childhood." In Israel, Elkayam's grandmother "kept the rhythms of her pastoral life in Morocco, waking at 5 a.m., making bread every day and socializing with other Moroccan exiles."[214]

When Morocco (together with Algeria and Tunisia) was ruled by Nazi-controlled Vichy France during World War II, Sultan Mohammed V resisted enforcing anti-Jewish laws. He told French officials, "I absolutely do not approve of the new anti-Semitic laws and I refuse to associate myself with a measure I disagree with. I reiterate as I did in the past that the Jews are under my protection and I reject any distinction that should be made amongst my people."[215] Mohammed V, although anti-Zionist, also sought to calm anti-Israel and anti-Jewish

---

214 Aida Alami, "Bridging Time, Distance and Distrust, With Music," *The New York Times*, March 26, 2021 https://www.nytimes.com/2021/03/26/world/middleeast/israel-singer-elkayam-morocco.html (accessed March 27, 2021).

215 Richard Hurowitz, "You Must Remember This: Sultan Mohammed V Protected the Jews of Casablanca," *Los Angeles Times*, April 25, 2017 https://www.latimes.com/opinion/op-ed/la-oe-hurowitz-moroccan-king-mohammed-v-20170425-story.html (accessed March 5, 2021). Some scholars argue that Mohammed V's protection of Moroccan Jews has been exaggerated. See Sophie Wagoner, "Contested Narratives: Contemporary Debates on Mohammed V and the Moroccan Jews Under the Vichy Regime," *Quest. Issues in Contemporary Jewish History*, November 2012 https://www.quest-cdecjournal.it/contested-narratives-contemporary-debates-on-mohammed-v-and-the-moroccan-jews-under-the-vichy-regime/ (accessed March 5, 2021). Lyn Julius is highly skeptical—see note 210, pp. 138–9. Julius in general believes that Jews in all Arab lands, including Morocco, were very badly treated for centuries.

sentiments of Moroccans when Israel was founded and its army was fighting Arab armies. In May 1948, he said that the only goal of Arab armies was to defend Jerusalem "and to re-establish peace and justice in the Holy Land, while preserving for the Jews the status that has always been accorded them since the Muslim conquest." He said, "the Moroccan Israelites who have lived for centuries in this country which has protected them, where they have found the best welcome, and where they have shown their complete devotion to the Moroccan throne, are different from the rootless Jews who have turned from the four corners of the earth towards Palestine, which they want to seize unjustly and arbitrarily." [216] Of course, the phrase "rootless Jews," reminiscent of Stalin's use of the phrase "cosmopolitan Jews," carries much with it.

Mohammed V's son, King Hassan II, who ascended the throne in 1961, often protected Morocco's Jews, in particular following domestic riots after Israel's victory in the 1967 Six-Day War. Hassan's son and Mohammed V's grandson, the reigning monarch King Mohammed VI, who became King in 1999, often refers approvingly to his grandfather's attitude to Jews. Mohammed VI has expressed friendliness towards Jews, and has set about restoring Morocco's synagogues, Jewish cemeteries and neighbourhoods, including those of Fez. In 2020, he approved a decision to teach Jewish history and culture as part of the Arabic-language curriculum in public primary schools. A statement from the American Sephardi Federation and the Conference of Presidents of Major American Jewish Organizations called this decision an "enduring commitment to recognizing a pluralist past" and said, "at the core of this effort is enhancing understanding and fostering the connection between Muslims and Jews."[217] Many of Morocco's museums exhibit items from its Jewish history. The 2011 constitution states that

---

216 See Gilbert, note 89, p. 225–6.
217 See U.S. Department of State, *2020 Report on International Religious Freedom: Morocco*, May 12, 2021 https://www.state.gov/reports/2020-report-on-international-religious-freedom/morocco/ (accessed May 22, 2021).

Jews are part of the national identity (Christians do not have this status). Jewish schools and synagogues receive government subsidies. A Jewish Culture Museum is scheduled to open in Fez. The University of Al-Quaraouiyine in Fez offers courses on the history of Judaism, Hebrew culture and language, and the Old Testament. Mohammed VI has normalized diplomatic relations and travel between Morocco and Israel. Direct flights between the two countries began in 2021. About one million Jews of Moroccan origin live in Israel, and officials from the two countries predict that large numbers of Israelis will visit Morocco.[218] In July 2022, the King authorized the establishment of new representative Jewish organizations—a National Council of the Moroccan Jewish Community, a Foundation of Moroccan Judaism with the task with protecting the community's heritage, and a Commission of Moroccan Jews Abroad—and acknowledged the Jewish tradition as a component of the Moroccan culture.

TURKEY

Jews have lived in what is now Turkey for more than two thousand years. The oldest community, now gone in Turkey but with remnants left in Greece, was the Greek-speaking Romaniote Jews. In the early 15th century, Ashkenazi Jews came to the Ottoman Empire from Germany and France. At the end of the 15th century, the Jewish population in Turkey was dramatically increased by Jews expelled from Spain and Portugal who were actively recruited as immigrants by the Ottoman Empire. After this Sephardic migration Jews made up 10 per cent or more of the population of Constantinople (now Istanbul). The port city of Salonica (now called Thessaloniki and part of Greece) was the

218 Not everyone has a rosy view of the modern Moroccan attitude towards Jews. See Ian Pokres, "Jews in Morocco Today: Not as Nice as You've Heard," *The Times of Israel*, March 31, 2021 https://blogs.timesofisrael.com/jews-in-morocco-today-not-as-nice-as-youve-heard/ (accessed March 31, 2021).

only city in the world where a plurality, and perhaps the majority, of the population was Jewish. It was known as the Jerusalem of the Balkans, and had more than fifty synagogues. The Jewish population of Salonica was overwhelmingly Sephardic, speaking Ladino, a mix of medieval Castilian and Hebrew. When Salonica became part of Greece in 1912, as a result of the First Balkan War between the Balkan League and the Ottoman Empire, there was a drive to Hellenize the city and the situation of Jews in the city took a turn for the worse. Many of Salonica's Jews emigrated to France or Palestine. Almost all of those who remained in Salonica became victims of Nazi genocide after Nazi Germany invaded Greece in 1941; they were deported to Auschwitz where they met their death.[219] Jews from Salonica who had gone to France were in due course rounded up by the Nazis and suffered the same fate. By 1943, there were virtually no Jews in Salonica.

Tolerated, with the status of *dhimmi*, Jews of the Ottoman Empire lived for the most part in peace and considerable prosperity for many years, subject to few restrictions, and enjoying considerable internal autonomy. Turkish Jews saw it as preferable to live under Muslim rule than Christian rule.[220] At the end of the 19th century, what is now Turkey was home to about 250,000 Jews. Some of these had fled from Russian pogroms in the late 19th century, joining other Ashkenazi Jews and descendants of those who had been expelled from Spain and Portugal centuries before. As Bernard Lewis commented, Jews were attracted by the reports they had heard about the greater tolerance and greater opportunity offered by the Ottoman government.[221]

In 1923, the Ottoman Empire, defeated on every front in World War I, was partitioned by the victors and replaced by the Turkish Republic, supposedly secular, and other successor states. A steady Jewish

---

219 For a poignant account of the fate of one Jewish family in Salonica, see Sarah Abrevaya Stein, *Family Papers: A Sephardic Journey Through the Twentieth Century* (New York: Picador, 2019).
220 See Phyllis Goldstein, note 20, p. 152.
221 Lewis, note 92, p. 121.

emigration began from the new Republic to the Palestine Mandate. This emigration was encouraged by the rejection of multiculturalism by Kemal Ataturk, the founding president of Turkey ("Turkification"), a new disdain for minorities who were suspected of disloyalty (although Ataturk sometimes professed a high regard for Jews), Nazi-inspired anti-Jewish laws adopted during World War II, and deteriorating economic circumstances. When the State of Israel was created, coinciding with the rise of the Turkish Islamist movement, the pace of emigration accelerated. Meanwhile, a new antisemitism had developed in Turkey, "the widely held belief that the collapse of the Ottoman Empire, the establishment of the secular Turkish Republic, and the creation of Israel were all part of a vast Jewish plot to weaken Islam, the Muslims, and the mighty Turkish nation."[222]

Today less than 20,000 Jews remain in Turkey, almost all in Istanbul. The number is a fraction of what was once there, but is still the largest concentration of Jews in a Muslim land. Franklin Hugh Adler describes this community as "a relic not only of what had been a central component of the distinctively Ottoman mosaic, but, more tragically, all that is left of the Jewish presence in Levantine society, from North Africa through Asia Minor, where Jews also had been a vital and permanent feature in the social, economic and cultural landscape."[223] The community continues to dwindle, with Turkish Jews still regularly leaving for Israel, and, in recent times, the United States. The Turkish state has become increasingly Islamic and anti-Israel, particularly under the leadership of President Recep Tayyip Erdoğan, although in December 2021, meeting with a delegation of Jewish leaders, Erdoğan spoke about

---

222 Rifat Bali, "The Slow Disappearance of Turkey's Jewish Community," January 6, 2011 Jerusalem Center for Public Affairs https://jcpa.org/article/the-slow-disappearance-of-turkeys-jewish-community/ (accessed April 27, 2021). And see Matt Kelly, "Student's Research Examines Jews' Role in Modern Turkish History," *UVAToday,* April 15, 2022 https://news.virginia.edu/content/students-research-examines-jews-role-modern-turkish-history (accessed April 20, 2022).

223 Franklin Hugh Adler, "Jews in Contemporary Turkey," *Macalester International* 15 (2005) pp. 127–8 http://digitalcommons.macalester.edu/macintl/vol15/iss1/13 (accessed April 26, 2021).

his desire to mend relations with Israel and said that antisemitism was a crime against humanity. At that meeting, Erdoğan stressed the importance of an Israeli effort to advance peace with the Palestinians.[224] In August 2022 Israel and Turkey restored full diplomatic relations and exchanged ambassadors.

EGYPT

Not so long ago there was a large, thriving, urban, middle-class, influential, and cosmopolitan Egyptian Jewish community.[225] In 1948 it numbered about 75,000. Now almost no Jews remain—perhaps five in Cairo and ten in Alexandria.[226] Writing in 1973, Jacqueline Shohet Kahanoff, a Jew and self-described "Levantine" born in Egypt, wrote "Once we had left Egypt, it broke our hearts to think . . . that a whole community, one of the most complex and interesting, disappeared without leaving a trace."[227] Egypt's Jews were a mix of so-called "indigines" who spoke Arabic as a mother tongue and claimed residence from the pre-Islamic era, Sephardi who had been expelled from Spain and Portugal, Jews from other parts of the Ottoman Empire who came for business opportunities

224 "Erdogan Tells Visiting Rabbis Ties with Israel Are 'Vital' for Regional Stability," *The Times of Israel* December 23, 2021 https://www.timesofisrael.com/erdogan-tells-visiting-rabbis-ties-with-israel-are-vital-for-regional-stability/ (accessed December 27, 2021).

225 For some insight into this complicated world, and its eventual collapse, see Jacqueline Shohet Kahanoff, note 91.

226 See Declan Walsh and Ronen Bergman, "A Bittersweet Homecoming for Egypt's Jews," *The New York Times*, February 23, 2020 https://www.nytimes.com/2020/02/23/world/middleeast/a-bittersweet-homecoming-for-egypts-jews.html (accessed May 17, 2021).

227 Note 91, p. 118. Kahanoff was lamenting that almost no one had told the story of Egypt's Levantine population. She writes that "the one significant work about Egypt's Levantine world, the *Alexandria Quartet*, was written . . . by Lawrence Durrell, an Irishman." In this context, "Levantine" refers to a Jew of multicultural heritage, for example a Sephardic Jew educated according to the European model, often in French (like Kahanoff), often with an ambivalent attitude towards Zionism.

after the Suez Canal opened in 1869, and, of course, Ashkenazi fleeing the Russian pogroms of the late 19th century. It is said that the Sephardi community, comprising the overwhelming majority of Egyptian Jews, imbued with French culture, educated in French, and for the most part speaking French among themselves, regarded the Ashkenazim as social inferiors,[228] the reverse of the attitudes in Israel at the founding of that State.

The position of Egyptian Jews deteriorated when Egypt became independent in 1922 and a British presence no longer mitigated extreme views. It deteriorated further with the growth of Zionism (regarded with hostility by the Egyptian government, although it seems that not many Egyptian Jews were Zionists), the influence of Nazi Germany, and the 1948 Arab–Israeli War, in which Egypt participated—in other words, for political and related reasons, and not because of religious difference or persecution. As a result of all these influences, economic, administrative, and political discrimination against Jews grew throughout the post-independence period. Anti-Jewish riots became commonplace in Cairo. By 1950 almost 40 per cent of Egyptian Jews had emigrated, mostly to Israel, but some to France and elsewhere. Another mass emigration followed the 1956 Suez Crisis. The rest of the Egyptian Jewish community, by then tiny, effectively disappeared following the Six-Day War of 1967, its members deported or jailed. Beinin writes, "By the time of Anwar al-Sadat's visit to Jerusalem in November 1977, an entire generation of Egyptians had matured having never personally seen or known a Jew. They often had great difficulty imagining Jews as members of the Egyptian national community."[229] Today, the government of Egypt claims to be rescuing Jewish synagogues and cemeteries "so Jewish heritage can take its rightful place alongside Egypt's Pharaonic, Coptic and Islamic civilizations."[230] But it remains the case, with Egypt as all Muslim countries, almost nobody knows an

228 See Beinin, note 194.
229 Beinin, note 194.
230 See Walsh and Bergman, note 226.

actual Jew, and impressions and attitudes develop from uncurated and corrupt social media.

CODA: KYRGYZSTAN

Our plane from Istanbul to Bishkek, the capital of Kyrgyzstan, once a station on the Silk Road, arrived in the middle of the night. Kyrgyzstan was part of the Soviet Union and remains in the Russian orbit. As we approached the Bishkek airport, I looked out of the window down at the ground below and saw only complete darkness. It was hard to believe that a city lay beneath us. Through the centuries wandering Jews have tried to find a home in this small and distant Central Asian country, as almost everywhere else in the world.

The Jewish history of Kyrgyzstan is kaleidoscopic. Jewish traders from Iran and other places, travelling along the Silk Road, visited, and some settled, in the 6th century. By the 10th century there were several towns with Jewish populations. Later, in the 19th and early 20th centuries, Jews came from Russia. There were never many in Kyrgyzstan, except once. During World War II, more than 20,000 Jews fled from Nazi-occupied western parts of the Soviet Union to Kyrgyzstan, swelling a small community to almost 40,000.[231] Synagogues opened in the cities of Bishkek, Osh, and Kant. But in the latter part of the 20th century most Kyrgyzstan Jews left for Israel, particularly following an unexplained and unusual antisemitic outbreak in 2010. Today it is estimated that less than 2,000 remain, almost all living in Bishkek.

---

231 This also happened in Uzbekistan. See Sharon Lurye, "Letter from Bukhara: Finding the Last Vestiges of Community in Central Asia's Jewish Heartland," *The Calvert Journal* August 26, 2021 https://www.calvertjournal.com/features/show/13061/letter-from-bukhara-jewish-central-asia-uzbekistan-history (accessed September 11, 2021). And see Christian Mamo, "Bukhara's Jewish Community Ensures Despite Emigration," *Emerging Europe*, September 18, 2021 https://emerging-europe.com/after-hours/bukharas-jewish-community-endures-despite-emigration/ (accessed September 18, 2021). There are less than a thousand Jews in Uzbekistan today. The New York area is home to an estimated 80,000 Jews of Bukharan descent.

We stayed for a week in Bishkek, attending a PEN International Congress. At the airport, to catch a plane back to Istanbul, anxious to leave this drab and unfriendly city, I faced an unsmiling passport control officer wearing a military uniform with a Russian-style peaked hat. He looked at my passport photo and then studied my face, with a slight hint of menace. He did this several times. My nervousness increased. Then the officer waved me through and I gladly left Kyrgyzstan for Turkey.

CHAPTER 4

JEWS AND CHRISTIANS

THE JEW AS ENEMY

The 2020 Pew survey of American Jews reported that nearly 40 per cent of U.S. Jews feel they have something in common with Muslims. Fewer said they have anything in common with evangelical Christians.[232] The reason for this is not clear, but perhaps it is the residue of history. As we have seen, through the centuries the relationship between Jews and Muslims has often been friendly and cooperative, if not intimate. In our time, relations are at a low point, poisoned principally by the political issue of Palestine. That may pass as a long and better history asserts itself. Muslims have no fundamental philosophical or theological grievance against Jews. But this is not the case with Christians. The aggressive and largely hostile attitude of Christians towards Jews has been propelled by an ancient family rift and by the myth of Jewish deicide. No wonder Jews are wary of their Christian brothers. No wonder that some Jews prefer the company of Muslims to the company of Christians.

232 Note 108.

"There's not much new in the New Testament. It grows out of the Hebrew scriptures," so says Giles Fraser, one-time Dean of St. Paul's in London.[233] Many others have said something similar. Some argue that modern Christianity is not much more than ancient Judaism warmed up.[234] Jews may not accept the New Testament, but Christians accept the Old Testament. Jesus, a Jew of intense spirituality,[235] taught his disciples how to read old scriptures in new ways: renewal, not replacement, was his purpose. The apostle Paul, also a Jew, gave the details of this mission in his epistles. For Paul, "the category of Jew, of descendant of Abraham, is not overcome or rendered immaterial, but rather appropriated and refined . . ."[236] Karen Armstrong writes, "During the first century, Christians continued to think about God and pray to him like Jews; they argued like Rabbis, and their churches were similar to the synagogues."[237] But, as is so often the case, familial closeness and breach of that close relationship was fertile soil for bitterness and

233 From BBC Arts & Ideas, "Links Between Judaism and Christianity" (an interview with Giles Fraser) https://podcasts.apple.com/ca/podcast/arts-ideas/id140685432?i= 1000518980691 (accessed May 24, 2021).

234 Bernard Lewis points out the "common endeavour" in the early days between the three great monotheistic religions. He gives as an example "a chapter in one of the theological writings of the great Muslim theologian al-Ghazālī (1059–1111) that is almost identical to a chapter in a work by his near contemporary, the Jewish philosopher Bahye ibn Paquda" and points out that both had their source in an earlier work by a Christian. See Bernard Lewis, note 92, pp. 56–57.

235 The description of Jesus as a Jew is complicated. See Carroll, note 2, ch. 9. Carroll's influential book was a bestseller, but engendered criticism and controversy. In *The New York Times,* Andrew Sullivan called it "a rigorous theological and moral dialectic": see "Christianity's Original Sin," January 14, 2001 https://archive.nytimes. com/www.nytimes.com/books/01/01/14/reviews/010114.14sullivt.html (accessed June 20, 2021). But a review by Ruth Langer called it a "massive oversimplification" although conceding that his "basic narrative is fundamentally correct." See *CCAR Journal: A Reform Jewish Quarterly* XLVIII:3 (Summer 2001): 9. In another review, Philip Cunningham wrote, "Carroll's numerous theological claims are often overstated, overreaching, or poorly substantiated." See *SIDIC Review* 34/2: 28–31. The Langer and Cunningham reviews can be found at https://www.bc.edu/content/ dam/files/research_sites/cjl/texts/cjrelations/resources/reviews/Constantines_ Sword.htm#Philip%20A.%20Cunningham's%20review (accessed June 20, 2021).

236 David Nirenberg, note 14, p. 56.

237 *A History of God* (New York: Ballantine Books, 1993), p. 90.

rivalry. This was not unique to Christians and Jews. As noted earlier, David Nirenberg has argued that, similarly, the early Muslims "sought to appropriate the prophetic traditions of Judaism while at the same time distancing itself from them."[238] But, as Bernard Lewis has written, "the conflict between Christians and Jews had that special bitterness that often makes conflicts within religions more deadly than those between religions."[239]

The "Jesus movement" quickly became "a vastly gentile church independent of Jews and their synagogues . . ."[240] Any vestige of familial closeness between Jews and Christians disappeared. Gospel authors— John, for example, writing towards the end of the 1st century—took a grim view of Jews and Judaism. They stressed that enmity for Jews and Judaism was a necessity for Christians and Christianity. After all, Jews did not accept Christ's divinity. Jews believed that only God was God (no Trinity for them) and that accordingly the Messiah could not be divine. Most important of all, they had killed Jesus, a monstrous crime. Deicide by the Jews became a core idea of the Christian church. Bernard Lewis observes that many of those who distrusted and oppressed Jews believed they were doing God's work.[241] Christianity became defined, in part, in opposition to Judaism.

Increasingly Christianity saw itself as universal and exclusive. It preached that Jesus Christ was the only way to salvation. There was no room for Jews (or anyone else) who disagreed. Jews came to be regarded as heretics who should if possible be converted and if necessary be tortured and subjected to inquisition. Giles Fraser writes that Christianity and Judaism "once so close as to be almost indistinguishable, turned against each other painfully and acrimoniously and came to live semi-separate lives, the separation disrupted only by intense periods of persecution—by

238 Note 14, p. 164.
239 Note 17.
240 David Nirenberg, note 14, p. 86.
241 Note 25, p. 101.

Christians against Jews."[242] In his book *Constantine's Sword*, James Carroll, a devout Catholic and former priest, writes, "Catholic medieval absolutism exacerbated anti-Jewish religious hatred, fueled new levels of violence, and sponsored an ever more hysterical conversionism, which, when up against continued Jewish resistance, finally led to modern anti-semitic racism."[243] Carroll adds that Catholic contempt for Jews through the centuries "was largely a response to an imagined Judaism. There was little authentic interaction between Jewish communities and the Church. From early on, "the Jews" were defined by Christians far more in terms of the anachronistic categories of the Old Testament than of the living and changing traditions of Jewish culture . . ."[244]

As Christianity became defined by opposition to Judaism, so, in a familiar pattern, the identity of Jews became shaped by the hatred that surrounded them. They turned inward. "The Jews distance themselves from their non-Jewish environment, become suspicious and mistrustful of attempts at rapprochement, particularly since these often turn out to be hidden attempts at conversion. The Jews turn inside, engage in Talmudic study and—hope against hope—long for deliverance."[245] Or, as Shlomo Sand puts it, "law and power forced Jews to retrench behind the gates of their faith."[246]

In October 1965, Pope Paul VI and the Second Vatican Council, in the conciliar declaration known as *Nostra Aetate*, officially repudiated the accusation that the Jews killed Jesus. But the repudiation was carefully hedged: "True, the Jewish authorities and those who followed their lead pressed for the death of Christ; still, what happened in His passion cannot be charged against all the Jews, without distinction,

---

242 *Chosen: Lost and Found Between Christianity and Judaism* (Great Britain: Allen Lane, 2021) p. 123.

243 Note 2, p. 318.

244 Note 2, p. 19.

245 Yakov Rabkin, "'A Wandering People-race'—Shlomo Sand's New Book on Judéophobia," *Mondoweiss*, August 4, 2021 https://mondoweiss.net/2021/08/a-wandering-people-race-shlomo-sands-new-book-on-judeophobia/. This is a review of Shlomo Sand, *Une Race Imaginaire* (Paris: Seuil, 2020).

246 Note 29, p. 28.

then alive, nor against the Jews of today."[247] It seems to me that this repudiation was half-hearted and a bit late, to say the least.

CHRISTIANITY AND THE HOLOCAUST

Some argue that Christian repudiation of Jews over almost two millennia helped lay the groundwork for the Holocaust (others, of course, vigorously repudiate this suggestion). James Carroll links "ancient Christian hatred of Jews to the twentieth century's murderous hatred that produced the death camps . . ."[248] He writes, "However modern Nazism was, it planted its roots in the soil of age-old Church attitudes and a nearly unbroken chain of Church-sponsored acts of Jew hatred. However pagan Nazism was, it drew its sustenance from groundwater poisoned by the Church's most solemnly held ideology—its *theology*."[249] Some parts of the Christian church are sensitive to accusations of this kind. The Church of England has formally recognized that centuries of Christian antisemitism contributed to the Holocaust. A 2019 Church of England document on Christian–Jewish relations concluded, "the theological teachings of the Church have in fact 'compounded the spread of the virus' of antisemitism. The attribution of collective guilt to the Jewish people for the death of Christ and the consequent interpretation of their suffering as collective punishment sent by God is one very clear example of that. Within living memory, such ideas contributed to fostering the passive acquiescence if not positive support of many Christians in actions that led to the Holocaust."[250] In 2022, in

---

247 See Catholic Church England and Wales, "Nostra Aetate," February 1, 2022 https://www.cbcew.org.uk/nostra-aetate/ (accessed April 19, 2022).

248 Note 2, p. 16.

249 Note 2, p. 477.

250 See Faith and Order Commission, *God's Unfailing Word: Theological and Practical Perspectives on Christian-Jewish Relations* (London: Church House Publishing, 2019). https://www.churchofengland.org/sites/default/files/2019-11/godsunfailingwordweb.pdf (accessed May 9, 2022), p. xiv.

an eccentric follow-up, the Church of England formally apologized for passing anti-Jewish laws in the 13ᵗʰ century which led to the expulsion of all Jews from England.

Supersessionism is a particularly dangerous form of Christian antisemitism. Sometimes called replacement theology, it is the specific idea that followers of Jesus replaced the Jews as the chosen people of God, and that Christianity, a newer covenant, is a far better religion than Judaism, which was merely a prologue to Christianity.[251] "Replacement" easily implies the elimination of those who have been replaced, whether it be by conversion, expulsion, or even genocide; after all, those who have been replaced are inferior people of no consequence and it matters not at all what happens to them. Replacement theology has also been used to deny that the Jewish people have any ancestral claim to the Land of Israel. How could they have such a claim, if they have been supplanted by Christians?

Daniel Goldhagen, in his controversial and brilliant book *Hitler's Willing Executioners*,[252] does not pull his punches. He writes, "European antisemitism is a corollary of Christianity. From the earliest days of Christianity's consolidation of its hold over the Roman Empire, its leaders preached against Jews, employing explicit, powerfully worded, emotionally charged condemnations." Supersessionism was part of this logic. Christianity was conceived as superseding Judaism and therefore "Jews as Jews ought to disappear from the earth."[253] If Jews were right in their theology, then Christians were wrong, and that could not be the case. Goldhagen writes that from the early days of Christianity antagonisms towards Jews "were embedded in the theological and

251 On the issue of whether Christianity is a "better" religion, and the interpretation of New Testament text that suggests it is, see Jesper Svartvik, "The New Testament's Most Dangerous Book for Jews," *The Christian Century*, September 13, 2021 https://www.christiancentury.org/article/critical-essay/new-testament-s-most-dangerous-book-jews (accessed September 13, 2021).
252 Note 31.
253 Note 31, p. 49.

psychological fabric of Christianity."[254] These attitudes endured into modernity. They culminated during the Nazi years, with both Protestant and Catholic churchmen embracing virulent antisemitism, and promoting the Holocaust.[255] "The conception of Jews as being violators of the moral order of the world was an axiom of Christian cultures."[256] As violators of the moral order, Jews deserved no mercy. (This is not to gainsay that, during the Nazi period, many ordinary Christians and churchmen tried to help persecuted Jews, often putting themselves in peril.)

Goldhagen makes the point that the enmity of German Christian churches towards the Jews was not just a traditional religious enmity but had a racist overlay. Until recent times racism has been the handmaiden of virulent antisemitism. Racism negates conversion; you can change your religion, you can pretend to be a Christian, but you cannot change your race. The enmity of German churchmen was also cultural and political. They saw Jews as a race who were "the principal driving force behind the relentless tide of modernity that was steadily eroding hallowed and time-honored values and traditions. They held Jews to be promoters of mammonism, of 'soulless capitalism,' of materialism, of liberalism, and, above all, of that skeptical and iconoclastic temper that was seen as the bane of the age."[257] Accordingly, they watched in silence, sometimes with approval, the suffering inflicted on the Jews by Germans. Of course, aversion to a dangerous modernity allegedly promoted by Jews was not unique to German Christianity. We have already referred to this phenomenon—the embrace of antisemitism as a politically convenient hatred. Aversion to modernity pops up as a hatred of Jews.

Supersessionism lives on as a theory, even at the highest ecclesiastical levels. In August 2021 Pope Francis reflected on Paul's teaching about

254 Note 31, pp. 50–51.
255 Note 31, pp. 107–14.
256 Note 31, p. 52.
257 Note 31, p. 436.

Torah. He said: "God offered them [the Jewish people] the Torah, the Law, so they could understand his will and live in justice. We have to think that at that time, a Law like this was necessary, it was a tremendous gift that God gave his people." But later, in the same reflections, the Pope said: "The Law, however, does not give life, it does not offer the fulfillment of the promise because it is not capable of being able to fulfill it. The Law is a journey, a journey that leads toward an encounter . . . Those who seek life need to look to the promise and to its fulfillment in Christ." These insensitive and damaging comments, seemingly oblivious to the profound implications of supersessionism and its effect throughout history, were met with consternation by some Jews who saw them as denigrating Judaism. Rabbi Daniel Polish wrote of the Pope's catechesis: "It speaks in the too-familiar language of disdain for Torah, dismissive of that which is most precious to his Jewish interlocutors. And it lends credence to those voices in the Jewish community who were unpersuaded by 'Nostra Aetate.' It suggests that despite all that has flowed from Vatican II, all the meetings, all the statements and all the progress, the notion of full reciprocity has still not been fully embraced at the highest levels of the church. It suggests that despite 'Nostra Aetate' and all the understanding that has flowed from it, somewhere in the innermost thinking of the church the idea of replacement theology still dominates. That the pope could embrace the notion that Torah is just a way-station to a fuller, higher truth is painful to Jewish ears."[258]

258 Daniel F. Polish, "Why Pope Francis' Comments on the Torah Were Hurtful to His Jewish Friends," *America: The Jesuit Review*, September 8, 2021 https://www. americamagazine.org/faith/2021/09/08/pope-francis-judaism-theology-241356 (accessed September 9, 2021).

CODA: EVANGELICAL CHRISTIANITY

There are about 700 million evangelical Christians in the world, with about 100 million in the United States. In a strange twist, many of them, particularly those in the United States, and particularly those who are older, are strong supporters of Israel. Many regard the establishment of a Jewish state as fulfillment of divine prophecy. As the American historian Walter Russell Mead writes, "For hundreds of millions of evangelical and Pentecostal Christians in the United States and beyond, the rise of Israel is seen to prove the truth of salvationist Christianity in the real world."[259] A 2021 survey found that just over half of American evangelical Christians believe that the Jews are God's chosen people, although only 20 per cent of those surveyed put a very high priority on supporting the Jewish people and Israel.[260]

Many evangelicals consider a Palestinian state, and the relinquishing by Israel of any occupied territory, as contrary to God's plan.[261] This view makes them popular in certain circles. These evangelicals have been influential in Washington, particularly when Donald Trump was president. They still have considerable influence, especially in the Republican party. The former Israeli ambassador to the United States, Ron Dermer, said when leaving office, in May 2021, "People have to understand that the backbone of Israel's support in the United States is the evangelical Christians. It's true because of numbers and also because of their passionate and unequivocal support for Israel.

259 Note 93, p. 440.
260 Tony Davenport, "How Many Evangelicals Believe Jews Are God's Chosen People?" *Vision*, December 27, 2021 https://vision.org.au/radio/news/how-many-evangelicals-believe-jews-are-gods-chosen-people/ (accessed December 27, 2021). For a different emphasis, see Jason Silverman, "New Survey Exposes Evangelical Support for Israel as Exaggerated," *Israel Today*, December 29, 2021 https://www.israeltoday.co.il/read/new-survey-exposes-evangelical-support-for-israel-as-exaggerated/ (accessed January 2, 2021).
261 See Colum Lynch, "What's Next for Christian Zionists?" *Foreign Policy*, July 19, 2021 https://foreignpolicy.com/2021/07/19/christian-zionists-israel-trump-netanyahu-evangelicals/ (accessed August 2, 2021).

About 25 percent [of Americans]—some people think more—are evangelical Christians. Less than 2 percent of Americans are Jews. So if you look just at numbers, you should be spending a lot more time doing outreach to evangelical Christians than you would do to Jews."[262] Reportedly former Israeli Prime Minister Benjamin Netanyahu was of the same view. In 2017 Netanyahu, emphasizing values shared between American evangelicals and Israel and in particular religious freedom, "told a Christian evangelical audience in Washington on Monday that they were Israel's best friends in the world . . ."[263]

Evangelical Christians may support Israel and oppose a Palestinian state, but that doesn't mean they are keen on Judaism or like Jews. They may even be antisemitic. Giles Fraser argues that evangelicals are at bottom supersessionists. In the supersessionist mind "an old and tired Judaism gives way to the new and vigorous Christianity, as a parent does to its child . . . although Judaism is respected, there is no longer any need for it. Jews need to be converted to Christianity in order for God's plan to come to fruition."[264] Hence we have movements like "Jews for Jesus," supersessionism all over again.

262 "Ex-Ambassador Dermer: Israel Should Focus More on Outreach with Evangelicals," *JewishPress.com*, May 10, 2021 https://www.jewishpress.com/news/israel/ex-ambassador-dermer-israel-should-focus-more-on-outreach-with-evangelicals/2021/05/10/ (accessed July 30, 2021).
263 Rebecca Shimoni Stoil, "Netanyahu: Evangelical Christians Are Israel's Best Friends," *The Times of Israel*, July 18, 2017 https://www.timesofisrael.com/netanyahu-evangelical-christians-are-israels-best-friends/ (accessed August 2, 2021).
264 Fraser, note 242, pp. 123–4.

CHAPTER 5

JEWS AND ZIONISM

KASHMIR AND PALESTINE

In the summer of 1963, I was a University of Manitoba student delegate to the World University Service of Canada's seminar in Pakistan. Each delegate had to pick a Pakistan-related research topic. I chose "The Problem of Kashmir." The seminar delegates, from across Canada, assembled in New York on their way to Asia. While I was in New York, at the suggestion of Bill Hull, a political science professor of mine back home in Winnipeg, I went to talk to Leo Malania, then the highest ranking Canadian at the United Nations and a special assistant to U Thant, the U.N. Secretary-General. Malania received me with courtesy and kindness. He asked what I would be studying in Pakistan. I told him—the problem of Kashmir. There was a moment or two of silence. He looked out of his office window at the East River below. Then he said, "You might want to reconsider the word 'problem.' It suggests that there is a solution. Some problems have no solutions. In those cases, all we can do is manage the situation." Malania was right, certainly about Kashmir. Sixty years on, the "problem" of Kashmir remains.

There are other problems like this in the world, many of them. One is Palestine.[265] How do you manage the problem of Palestine? Is there a solution? It would be easy to say, no, there is no solution. Palestine is like Kashmir.[266] The best we can do is try and manage things. But attempts to manage the Palestine problem have failed dismally. They have created more and more instability and danger. More and more poison has been dumped into the well. More and more suffering has been inflicted. Should we attempt to go beyond management, imagine that there might be a solution, and look for it?

SETTLER COLONIALISM

Zionism and the modern history of Palestine fuel antisemitism as hydrogen fuels the Sun. There are no bigger drivers of Jew-hatred. To many, Zionism and Palestinian history exemplify "a colonial war waged against the indigenous population . . . to force them to relinquish their homeland to another people against their will."[267] These anti-Zionists see the history of Israel and its current policies as an example of

265 Today "Palestine" is generally taken to refer collectively to the West Bank and Gaza Strip, including those parts of the West Bank occupied by Israel. Another use of the term refers to the entire region between the Mediterranean Sea and the Jordan River, including what is now Israel.

266 I'm not the only one to bracket Kashmir and Palestine. In October 2021, the representative of Pakistan told the United Nations Security Council that "Middle East and adjacent regions will not witness durable peace so long as the people of Palestine and Kashmir continue to suffer under foreign occupation . . ." See "Peace Impossible if Palestine, Kashmir Disputes Remain Unresolved: Pakistan," *Pakistan Today*, October 20, 2021 https://www.pakistantoday.com.pk/2021/10/20/peace-impossible-if-palestine-kashmir-disputes-remain-unresolved-pakistan/ (accessed October 20, 2021). In February 2022, Redfish Media, a news agency with links to the Russian government, released a documentary entitled "Kashmir: Palestine in Making." See Nayanima Basu, "Russia 'State Agency' Film Equates Kashmir with Palestine, Moscow Goes into Damage-control," *The Print*, February 7, 2022 https://theprint.in/diplomacy/russia-state-agency-film-equates-kashmir-with-palestine-moscow-goes-into-damage-control/823603/ (accessed March 11, 2022).

267 Khalidi, note 104, p. 9.

so-called "settler colonialism." They condemn all Jews who support this history and these policies, be they in Israel or in the Diaspora. They call these Jews "Zionists." Sometimes anti-Zionists make an astonishing leap of illogic and condemn all Jews everywhere regardless of their views on these issues. To them, all Jews are Zionists (this is clearly not the case). To them, Zionists and Jews are one and the same. Then, anti-Zionism becomes antisemitism. To call someone a Zionist is to utter an antisemitic slur. Sometimes it seems that this aberrant form of antisemitism will never wither and die until the Palestinian conflict has been resolved, until the supply of hydrogen is cut off from the sun.

Can you be anti-Zionist but not antisemitic? Can you criticize the history and policies of Israel without being an antisemite, or, if you are Jewish, "self-hating"? The answer to both questions is unequivocally yes. Conflating anti-Zionism and antisemitism, insisting that all those opposed to Zionism must hate all Jews, calling anti-Zionism the "new antisemitism" or the "new political antisemitism" or "antisemitism masquerading as political critique" or "political-cum-ideological Judeophobia" or "concealed racism," is clearly wrong, although commonplace.[268] This conflation is often done for insidious political effect and advantage. Many Jews easily fall into this obvious trap, regarding as an antisemite anyone who is opposed to Zionism. Then there is the reverse but related question of whether you can be a Zionist, in the sense of being a supporter of Israel in general, but not a racist and supporter of settler colonialism. The answer to the question is again an unequivocal yes. It is another illogical conflation, as bad as the first, but perhaps more understandable, to consider any Zionist as necessarily a racist and supporter of settler colonialism. You can be a supporter of Israel without unequivocally supporting its history and endorsing egregious policies.

268 For example, Jonathan Greenblatt, director of the U.S. Anti-Defamation League, has repeatedly said "Anti-Zionism Is Anti-Semitism." See Isaac Chotiner, "Is Anti-Zionism Anti-Semitism?" *The New Yorker*, May 11, 2022 https://www.newyorker.com/news/q-and-a/is-anti-zionism-anti-semitism (accessed May 12, 2022). Greenblatt attempts to square the circle by nervously and defensively advocating for a two-state solution that would allow for Palestinian nationalism.

Zionism and the founding of the State of Israel, and the subsequent history of what is known as Palestine, have enormously complicated the analysis of antisemitism by intertwining racial and ethnic prejudice and geopolitical controversy. Equating anti-Zionism with antisemitism is often a way of sidestepping and obscuring the genuine grievances that Arabs and others have against Israel and impedes any progress towards resolving conflict. Anyone who sympathizes with these grievances and seeks a remedy is liable to being called an antisemite. The appalling history of antisemitism, culminating in the Holocaust, is wrongly used, like a magic wand, to justify thinking illogically. Peter Beinart has written, for example, of American Jewish organizations that they have stretched antisemitism's definition to the point of absurdity in their effort to inoculate Israel policy from criticism. "All too often, Jews assume ... that Jews, because of our history of persecution, can play fast and loose in the Israeli government's defense. This moral promiscuity constitutes a terrible abuse of the authority that Jewish leaders enjoy as a result of the history of Jewish suffering."[269]

Unlike other examples of so-called settler colonialism—white settlers in North America and the Antipodes, for example—Zionism purports to have historical and religious claims to the land ("Zionism appealed above all to the Bible, which it presented as a legal property title"[270]) and powerful moral entitlement derived from centuries of persecution culminating in the Holocaust. But, despite these claims and this moral entitlement, many consider that the ethical basis of Israel has been undermined by the displacement of an indigenous population and the subsequent unrelenting and disproportionate suppression of the descendants of that population, often by force. In any event, whatever the competing moral and other claims of Israelis and Palestinians may be, both peoples have shown great resilience and neither can now be vanquished. The way forward will not be found in victory for one and defeat of the other.

269 Note 28, p. 58.
270 Sand, note 29, p. 48.

THEODOR HERZL

Theodor Herzl—charismatic, depressed, lonely, and beautiful (so he was described by contemporaries, and photographs bear out this description)—created the political arm of the Zionist movement in 1896 with the publication of his famous (but dull) pamphlet *Der Judenstaat*.[271] It is interesting that it took so long for Jews to see the importance of organizing politically. Right from the start, more than a thousand years before, Mohammed knew it was essential, and proved himself to be, not just a charismatic religious leader, but also an astute politician and military man. But not all Jews saw the importance of independent political action. Herzl's ideas were unpopular with many Western Jews who thought they had assimilated into their local community and had no interest in Zionism upsetting the applecart.

Herzl's Zionism was encouraged by his presence as an Austrian journalist at the 1894 trial for treason of the Jewish French army officer Alfred Dreyfus (see Chapter 2). In 1897 Herzl convened the first World Zionist Congress, held in the municipal casino of Basle, Switzerland, to consider his views and proposals. There, in a Swiss casino, was born the World Zionist Organization. Herzl's purpose was to answer the so-called Jewish Question, that of the status of the Jews as a people in an age of raging political nationalism and new nation states. His vision

---

271 In translation, Theodor Herzl, *The Jewish State* (New York: Skyhorse Publishing, 2019). On Herzl, see Jacob de Haas, *Theodor Herzl: A Biographical Study* (Chicago: The Leonard Company, 1927). This two-volume biography was given to my father on his bar mitzvah, January 14, 1933, by the Bilmes family. Later that month Hitler became Chancellor of Germany. Another bar mitzvah guest gave my father Nahum Sokolow, *History of Zionism 1600–1918* (London: Longmans, Green, 1919). Sokolow (1860–1936) was General Secretary of the World Zionist Organization from 1905 to 1910 and was important in negotiating the Balfour Declaration. Family legend has it that Chaim Weizmann, the great Zionist who became first president of Israel, was a guest at my father's bar mitzvah, but I have been unable to verify that he was there. Weizmann was apparently a friend of my grandfather. A particularly good modern biography of Herzl is Derek Penslar, *Theodor Herzl: The Charismatic Leader* (New Haven: Yale University Press, 2020). Hannah Arendt said Herzl was a "crackpot," and possibly insane. See Linfield, note 26, p. 9.

was creation of a secular state that offered not only a refuge to Jews but also a secure and honoured place to Arabs and equal rights for women.[272] Herzl, I think, would be repelled by today's discriminatory treatment of Palestinians by Israel. He was not interested in religion; indeed, in the early days the Zionist movement was antireligious and inclusive of all faiths. He was not anti-Arab.

Herzl died in July 1904, in Vienna, at the age of forty-four. Stefan Zweig described his funeral grandiosely and perhaps inaccurately (it is doubtful that a million people attended):

> ... people arrived at all the Viennese railway stations, coming with every train by day and night, from all lands and countries; Western, Eastern, Russian, Turkish Jews—from all the provinces and small towns they suddenly stormed in ... the leader of a great movement was being carried to his grave ... There was uproar in the cemetery itself; too many mourners suddenly poured like a torrent up to his coffin, weeping, howling and screaming in a wild explosion of despair. There was an almost raging turmoil ... I could tell for the first time from all this pain, rising in sudden great outbursts from the hearts of a crowd a million strong, how much passion and hope this one lonely man had brought into the world by the force of his ideas.

ZIONISM AND THE CREATION OF ISRAEL

In the age of nationalism, beginning well before World War I, nation-states fervently pursuing a historical destiny (often trumped-up) began replacing colonial states, empires, and dynasties. Zionism asserted that Jews, too, were a nation. It followed that Jews, as a nation, required, and deserved, a state of their own. Zionism "transmuted the Jewish religion

272 Lewis, note 25, p. 176.

and the historic peoplehood of the Jews into something different—a modern nationalism . . ."[273] It demanded the establishment of a majority Jewish state in Palestine (after considering and rejecting other places, notably Argentina and Uganda[274]). It wanted Jews to be recognized as a nation like other nations. It ignored the fact that Palestine was part of the Ottoman Empire and the crucial fact that it had an indigenous population of almost a million people including some Jews who comfortably saw themselves as part of a Muslim-majority society. In 1914, Moshe Sharett, who was to become Israel's second prime minister, and also served as the country's foreign minister for eight years, said, "we have not come to an empty land to inherit it, but we have come to conquer a country from a people inhabiting it . . ."[275] Initially Zionism was smiled upon by some governments, particularly those of Germany and Russia, mostly because, disliking Jews, they were anxious for them to leave their countries and take up residence elsewhere. Zionism was opposed by many progressive and liberal Jews who saw the route to Jewish liberation as part of an overall social transformation rather than the transplanting of a population, and by some rabbinical authorities who "understood that Zionism represented, in the end, a collective assimilation into modernity, and that worship of the national soil, expressed in a new secular faith, would supplant devotion to the divine."[276]

273 Khalidi, note 104, p. 245.
274 "Herzl's Uganda Proposal Received Support from Unexpected Corners," *Intermountain Jewish News* March 11, 2021 https://www.ijn.com/herzls-uganda-proposal-received-support-from-unexpected-corners/ (accessed March 13, 2021). For a detailed account of this idea, see Eddy Mwanza, "Inside Plan to Create State of Israel in Western Kenya," https://www.kenyans.co.ke/news/65183-inside-plan-create-state-israel-western-kenya (accessed May 17, 2021). The Uganda Plan was officially rejected at the 1905 Seventh Zionist Congress.
275 See Allan C. Brownfeld, "Zionism's Original Sin: Ignoring the Fact That Palestine Was Fully Populated," *Washington Report on Middle East Affairs*, November/December 2021 https://www.wrmea.org/israel-palestine/zionisms-original-sin-ignoring-the-fact-that-palestine-was-fully-populated.html (accessed November 5, 2021).
276 Sand, note 29, pp. 75–76. And see David Finkel, "Why Do Socialists Oppose Zionism?" *International Viewpoint* September 2021 https://internationalviewpoint.org/spip.php?article7309 (accessed September 16, 2021).

The demands of a nation-state are many. One is a common language. A common language tends to unite the people who speak it. In the case of Zionism, a common language had to be imposed. As Shlomo Sand has pointed out, European Zionists were quick to discard Yiddish as their mother tongue: "The first thing they needed was a language that could unite Jews the world over . . . The early Zionists subsequently aspired to create a new Jew, who would break with the popular culture of their parents and ancestors as well as with the wretched townships of the pale of Settlement."[277] Hebrew, a language only used previously for religious rituals, was chosen as the new language. Yiddish, once the dominant language of Eastern European Jews and an essential part of its culture and identity, was sent into oblivion. In Mihail Sebastian's novel *For Two Thousand Years*, the character Abraham Sulitzer says of Yiddish: "It's a living language, with nerves and blood, with its own troubles, its own beauty. With its own homeland, which is the ghetto— the whole world, in other words. It makes me laugh when I hear those Zionists talking Hebrew picked up from books."[278] The same imperative applied to Sephardic Jews from North Africa who spoke Arabic but now had to learn Hebrew.

The idea of a Jewish nation is an example of an "imagined community" as explained by Benedict Anderson in his famous book about nationalism (Anderson also used the word "fantasy" to describe an imagined community).[279] Anderson defines a "nation" as an imagined political community, imagined as limited and sovereign. "It is *imagined* because the members of even the smallest nation will never know most of their fellow-members, meet them, or even hear of them, yet in the minds of each lives the image of their communion."[280] ("Fellow-members" covers a lot of ground. It includes those who are dead and those who are unborn.) A nation is limited because it has finite boundaries. It is

277 Sand, note 29, p. 41.
278 Note 95, p. 84.
279 Note 3.
280 Note 3, p. 6.

sovereign because nations dream of being free. It is a community because "the nation is always conceived as a deep, horizontal comradeship."[281] Anderson is careful to note that many of the members of an imagined community will love it and will even be prepared to die for it, despite the fact that they do not know, and know nothing about, almost all of the community's other members.

On November 2, 1917, the British government endorsed the creation of a Jewish homeland in Palestine in the Balfour Declaration, named after the British politician Arthur Balfour who, as foreign secretary, was the Declaration's main promoter.[282] The Balfour Declaration took on particular significance when the British almost immediately consolidated their military and political power over the Middle East (British forces commanded by General Allenby entered Jerusalem on December 11, 1917), replacing the Ottoman Empire, long in decline and ultimately defeated in World War I, as the region's ruler. The Declaration had a variety of motivations that went beyond a vague and romantic view of Jews, their history and destiny. Rashid Khalidi has argued that Britain's strategic interests were served by its sponsorship of "the Zionist project" and has also suggested there was an antisemitic wish to reduce Jewish immigration to Britain. (Balfour was thought to be personally antisemitic.) Theodor Herzl predicted that antisemites would be the best friends of Zionists and antisemitic countries would be their allies. That was because a far-off Jewish national homeland was a sanitary way to get rid of Jews living on your doorstep. Khalidi

281 Note 3, p. 7.
282 The Declaration was in the form of a letter to Lord Rothschild, honourary president of Britain's Zionist Federation. Its key sentence reads: "His Majesty's Government view with favour the establishment in Palestine of a national home for the Jewish people, and will use their best endeavours to facilitate the achievement of this object, it being clearly understood that nothing shall be done which may prejudice the civil and religious rights of existing non-Jewish communities in Palestine, or the rights and political status enjoyed by Jews in any other country." The Declaration was ambiguous and imprecise and—some argue—worded weakly intentionally. See, e.g., Milton Viorst, *Zionism: The Birth and Transformation of an Ideal* (New York: Thomas Dunne Books, 2016), pp. 85–88.

argues that Britain was also convinced that world Jewry "had the power to keep newly revolutionary Russia fighting in the war and bring the United States into it."[283] World Jewry had to be brought onside, and the Balfour Declaration was a way of doing it.

Following the Balfour Declaration, in the words of American historian Walter Russell Mead, a "flood of Jewish immigrants" built a "proto-state."[284] In 1922 the League of Nations adopted the Balfour Declaration and officially granted Britain the Palestine Mandate, making the principles of the Declaration legally binding and obliging Britain to pursue the policy of a Jewish national home, this latter, of course, opposed by Palestinian Arabs. That same year Britain carved Transjordan—the land east of the Jordan River—from Palestine and denied Jews the right to settle there: this still sticks in craw of staunch Zionists who see it as a betrayal. In 1937 a British Royal Commission of Inquiry, chaired by Lord Peel, proposed that Palestine be partitioned, with Palestinians being moved from areas designated for Jews. The legacy of the Peel Commission was the idea of a Palestinian population "transfer" (a euphemism if ever there was one) which benefitted Jews. Some argue that this idea made the Nakba (see below) historically and theoretically possible.

The Holocaust put Zionism in the forefront as both an answer to antisemitism and as just recompense and protection for the Jews who had suffered so much. On May 14, 1948, the Palestine Mandate ended, at the request and to the great relief of the war-weary British, theoretically leaving the problem of Palestine's future to be solved by the United Nations, which had been dithering on the issue for some time. Israel immediately and unilaterally declared its independence. Within days the armies of Israel's Arab neighbours advanced on the new state, beginning a war which lasted for almost a year. During this time, about 750,000 Arab Palestinians fled in the face of unrelenting Jewish military action or were expelled by Israel to adjacent lands in often brutal circumstances. The highly controversial Plan Dalet, implemented by

283   Note 104, p. 25.
284   Note 93, p. 239.

the Haganah, the predecessor of the Israeli Defence Force, led to the seizing and destruction of Arab villages and the expulsion of their inhabitants and, it is said, the murder and rape of many Arabs by Haganah forces. This drastic displacement of Palestinians is known as the Nakba, the Arabic word for disaster or catastrophe. Many of the descendants of those who experienced the Nakba are still living in camps near Israel, considered as refugees by some but not by all (the naysayers argue that "refugee status should not be handed down"). About 250,000 Palestinian refugees went to Gaza, turning it into one of the most densely populated and impoverished places in the world, and creating a centre of militant Palestinian activism.

At the end of the 1948 war, with Israel victorious, about 160,000 Arabs remained in that part of Palestine that was now Israel, living as "a despised minority in a hostile environment."[285] Descendants of those who remained in 1948, numbering about two million today—the so-called "Israeli Arabs"—officially have the same rights as Jewish Israelis. The Arab residents of East Jerusalem annexed by Israel in 1967, about 330,000 people, have a lesser status; almost all are classified as "permanent residents," not citizens, and cannot vote in Israeli elections or get Israeli passports. The West Bank, acquired from Jordan by conquest in 1967, has a population of about three million Arabs living a segregated life under a harsh Israeli military regime with little or no rights and, now, around 700,000 Jewish settlers in 130 settlements who have the full rights of Israeli citizens. Tom Friedman of *The New York Times* has written of the West Bank: "This occupation may not be the same as South African apartheid, but it is an ugly cousin and morally corrosive to Israel as a Jewish democracy. It is becoming so alienating to Israel's liberal friends, including the younger generations of American Jews, that, if it continues, Joe Biden may be the last pro-Israel Democratic president."[286] Gaza's population,

285 Khalidi, note 104, p. 83.
286 Tom Friedman, "Only Saudi Arabia and Israeli Arabs Can Save Israel as a Jewish Democracy," *The New York Times*, July 15, 2022 https://www.nytimes.

entirely Arab, is about two million (two-thirds of Gaza's people are under 25). And so, about the same number of Jews and Arabs—roughly seven million of each—live between the Jordan River and the Mediterranean Sea.

In 2018 Israel enacted a statute known as the Jewish Nation-State Law. It declared, among other things: Israel is the historic homeland of the Jewish people in which the State of Israel was established; the State of Israel is the nation-state of the Jewish people, in which it fulfills its natural, religious, and historic right to self-determination; the fulfillment of the right of national self-determination in the State of Israel is unique to the Jewish people; Hebrew is the language of the state; Israel is the historic homeland of the Jewish people in which the State of Israel was established; the state views Jewish settlement as a national value and will labor to encourage and promote its establishment and development.[287] There is no place for Arabs, even Israeli Arabs, in the Jewish Nation-State Law. The Law makes clear that nationality, not citizenship, is what counts in Israel. Omar Boehm has argued that specifying development of Jewish settlement as a national value puts in place the legal infrastructure for future annexations.[288]

ISRAEL AND PALESTINE

Zionism is now associated for many with the displacement and continuing misery of large numbers of Arabs. It is sometimes described as a racist movement. The treatment of Palestinians by Israel is often compared to the treatment of Blacks by the apartheid regime of South

com/2022/07/15/opinion/israel-saudi-arabia-biden-trip.html?referringSource= articleShare (accessed July 15, 2022).

287 For the full text of the Basic Law, see "Read the Full Jewish Nation-State Law," *The Jerusalem Post*, July 19, 2018 https://www.jpost.com/israel-news/read-the-full-jewish-nation-state-law-562923 (accessed September 30, 2021).

288 Omar Boehm, *Haifa Republic: A Democratic Future for Israel* (New York: New York Review of Books, 2021), p. 40.

Africa, for many an unfair and incendiary comparison. In 1997, Nelson Mandela, then president of South Africa, said "we know too well that our freedom is incomplete without the freedom of the Palestinians."[289] The late Desmond Tutu, former Archbishop of Cape Town and tireless campaigner against South African apartheid, often said the same thing. In January 2021, B'Tselem, a well-known and highly regarded (by some) Israeli organization monitoring human rights in the territories occupied by Israel, issued a detailed position paper describing the Israeli regime in the various areas under its control as an apartheid regime. The fact is, says the paper, "all Palestinians living under Israeli rule are treated as inferior in rights and status to Jews who live in the very same area."[290] This is indisputable. In April 2021, Human Rights Watch issued a report (controversial and much criticized) arguing "that Israel pursues a policy of ethnic supremacy that favors Israeli Jews over Palestinians in both Israel and the occupied territories."[291] The report also used the word "apartheid."[292] In February 2022, in a lengthy report, Amnesty International claimed that Israel maintains a

289 Address by President Nelson Mandela at International Day of Solidarity with Palestinian People, Pretoria, December 4, 1997 http://www.mandela.gov.za/mandela_speeches/1997/971204_palestinian.htm (accessed July 18, 2021).

290 B'Tselem, *A Regime of Jewish Supremacy from the Jordan River to the Mediterranean Sea: This Is Apartheid*, January 12, 2021 https://www.btselem.org/publications/fulltext/202101_this_is_apartheid (accessed July 29, 2021). See also Masha Gessen, "Why an Israeli Human-Rights Organization Decided to Call Israel an Apartheid Regime," *The New Yorker*, January 27, 2021 https://www.newyorker.com/news/our-columnists/why-an-israeli-human-rights-organization-decided-to-call-israel-an-apartheid-regime (accessed July 29, 2021).

291 See Patrick Kingsley, "Rights Group Hits Israel With Explosive Charge: Apartheid," *The New York Times*, April 27, 2021 https://www.nytimes.com/2021/04/27/world/middleeast/israel-apartheid-palestinians-hrw.html?referringSource=articleShare (accessed April 28, 2021).

292 *A Threshold Crossed: Israeli Authorities and the Crimes of Apartheid and Persecution*, Human Rights Watch, April 27, 2021 https://www.hrw.org/report/2021/04/27/threshold-crossed/israeli-authorities-and-crimes-apartheid-and-persecution (accessed April 28, 2021). For an attack on this report and other similar analyses, see Salo Aizenberg, "Essay: Critical Omissions," *Australia/Israel Review*, September 20, 2021 https://aijac.org.au/australia-israel-review/essay-critical-omissions/ (accessed September 23, 2021).

system of oppression and domination over Palestinians that constitutes a 'cruel apartheid.'[293]

Rashid Khalidi is a professor of Arab studies at Columbia University. He comes from a distinguished Palestinian family. He has been involved in Palestinian affairs for many years, and writes extensively on the Middle East. In 2020 he published a book called *The Hundred Years' War on Palestine: A History of Settler Colonialism and Resistance, 1917–2017.*[294] Khalidi describes the remarkable resilience of the Palestine cause over a long period of time, despite divided and largely incompetent Palestinian leadership and enormous well-organized opposition to the cause from Israel and elsewhere. He writes that, from the beginning, hard-line Zionists believed that if Palestine existed, Israel as a Jewish state could not. This belief was baked into Israeli thinking and public relations, and was expressed in uncompromising policies and the frequent use of disproportionate military force. Khalidi writes, "Since from the Zionist vantage point the name Palestine and the very existence of the Palestinians constituted a mortal threat to Israel, the task was to connect these terms indelibly, if they were mentioned at all, with terrorism and hatred, rather than with a forgotten but just cause."[295]

Hard-line Zionists, desirous of creating a Jewish state from the Jordan River to the Mediterranean Sea, subverted the idea of a two-state solution whenever possible in word and deed. On the other hand, the two-state solution idea was accepted (admittedly with varying degrees of commitment, enthusiasm, and nuance) by the Palestine Liberation Organization (PLO) and other Palestinian organizations for many years. The 1988 PLO Palestinian Declaration of Independence "formally abandoned the PLO's claim to the entirety of Palestine, accepting the

293 Amnesty International, *Israel's Apartheid against Palestinians: Cruel System of Domination and Crime Against Humanity*, February 1, 2022, https://www.amnesty.org/en/wp-content/uploads/2022/02/MDE1551412022ENGLISH.pdf (accessed April 19, 2022).

294 Note 104. Given the title and Khalidi's biography, it might be tempting to think of his book as pro-Palestinian special pleading. That would be a mistake.

295 Note 104, p. 117.

principles of partition, a two-state solution, and a peaceful resolution to the conflict . . . These were major political shifts for the PLO, the culmination of an evolution toward acceptance of Israel and of a Palestinian state alongside it that had begun in the early 1970s."[296] Later in 1988, the then head of the PLO, Yasser Arafat, formally recognized the right of Israel to exist in peace and security. In 2011, Mahmoud Abbas, PLO chairman and president of the Palestinian National Authority (created in 1994 by the Oslo Accords as a kind of Palestinian government-in-waiting, now more generally seen as a compliant agent of Israel's occupation) said, "We do not want to isolate Israel or to delegitimize it. On the contrary, we want to coexist with it."[297]

As time went by, faced with Israeli intransigence, and bedevilled by poor leadership and strategic mistakes, the PLO's importance diminished dramatically. It was eclipsed by Hamas, a militant outgrowth of the Palestinian branch of the Muslim Brotherhood. Violence by Palestinians became more acceptable as time went by. The second *intifada* or "uprising" (2000–2005) was considerably more violent than the first (1987–1991). Hamas formally took power in Gaza in 2006, winning legislative elections. A devastating Israeli blockade of Gaza, which continues to this day, followed. Khalidi is clear-eyed in his conclusions. "[T]here are now two peoples in Palestine, irrespective of how they came into being, and the conflict between them cannot be resolved as long as the national existence of each is denied by the other. Their mutual acceptance can only be based on complete equality of rights, including national rights, notwithstanding the crucial historical differences between the two."[298] Hamas leaders have said that if the Palestinian people vote to accept a two-state solution, it will agree.

Peter Beinart has a pedigree much different than Khalidi's. Beinart is an Orthodox Jew who attends synagogue regularly (like Khalidi, he lives

---

296 Note 104, p. 178.
297 See "Abbas: Palestinians Have No Wish to Isolate Israel," *Haaretz*, May 27, 2011 https://www.haaretz.com/1.5017119 (accessed July 25, 2021).
298 Note 104, p. 216.

in New York). He has been called "the most influential liberal Zionist of his generation."[299] He was a Rhodes Scholar and has been editor of *The New Republic*. He has become a figure of fierce controversy, often vilified and condemned by his fellow Jews, even berated on the street by irate Jewish passers-by who recognize him.[300] In 2012 Beinart published an influential book called *The Crisis of Zionism*.[301] Despite the differences between Khalidi and Beinart, the fact that one is a Palestinian and the other a Zionist, they share much ground. Herzl, writes Beinart, knew that Jews were entirely capable of birthing a Boer state. Beinart dwells on the conflict "between the desire to build a Jewish state premised on liberal democratic principles and the temptation to flout those principles in the name of Jewish security and power."[302] He stresses that we live in an age, not of Jewish weakness, but of Jewish strength "and that without moral vigilance, Jews will abuse power just as hideously as anyone else."[303] Furthermore, he argues, American Jewish leaders, in implicit alliance with Israeli leaders, are inclined to insist "that to even acknowledge the misuse of Jewish power was to deny Jewish victimhood and thus victimize Jews anew."[304]

But time is passing and attitudes are changing. In the United States, those who led the Jewish community for many years are dying off. Young American Jews think differently than their elders. Beinart argues that the young (or youngish) are far less likely to build their identity around victimhood. They are abandoning Zionism. Secular tribalism is in steep decline. He writes, "The harsh truth is that for

299 Benjamin Wallace-Wells, "A Liberal Zionist's Move to the Left on the Israeli-Palestinian Conflict," *The New Yorker*, May 23, 2021 https://www.newyorker.com/news/annals-of-populism/a-liberal-zionists-move-to-the-left-on-the-israeli-palestinian-conflict (accessed July 25, 2021).

300 E.g., see Yisrael Medad, "Terrible, Terrible Peter Beinart," *Jewish News Syndicate*, August 10, 2021 https://www.jns.org/opinion/terrible-terrible-peter-beinart/ (accessed August 12, 2021).

301 Note 28.

302 Note 28, p.13.

303 Note 28, p. 33.

304 Note 28, p. 38.

many young, non-Orthodox American Jews, Israel isn't that important because being Jewish isn't that important."[305] And they are unlikely to see Israel as a refuge: "Not only can they not imagine needing to flee to a Jewish state themselves . . . they see no significant community of Diaspora Jews that does."[306]

THE ONE-STATE SOLUTION

Beinart's thinking about Israel and Palestine has developed considerably since he wrote *The Crisis of Zionism*. He used to promote a two-state solution, but now advocates a single state, a secular binational state on all land between the Jordan River and the Mediterranean, fully protecting the rights of both Jews and Palestinians. The one-state solution has been gathering momentum, driven by new worldwide thinking on equality and human rights. In a detailed and compelling magazine article published in July 2020,[307] Beinart says it is clear that Jewish statehood as currently envisaged by Jewish leaders includes permanent Israeli control of the West Bank, and that Israeli leaders would not allow a Palestinian state to have sovereign powers. The two-state project is therefore impossible. The only alternative is one state in which Palestinians have equal rights.

The one-state idea is attracting increasing interest and support, in the United States and elsewhere, despite demographic implications seen as catastrophic by many Jews. How could a democratic Israel remain a Jewish state if there were as many, or more, Arabs in the country as Jews? Nonetheless, Beinart writes, "[T]he demand for equality—as manifested in the civil rights movement, the anti-apartheid movement,

---

305 Note 28, p. 169.
306 Note 28, p. 181.
307 Peter Beinart, "Yavne: A Jewish Case for Equality in Israel-Palestine," *Jewish Currents*, July 7, 2020 https://jewishcurrents.org/yavne-a-jewish-case-for-equality-in-israel-palestine/ (accessed July 26, 2021).

and the Black Lives Matter movement—retains enormous moral power." Bret Stephens writing in *The New York Times* is not impressed by Beinart's proposal of a single binational state. He described it as utopian in theory, bound to be disastrous if it were ever implemented, feckless, unworkable and unoriginal.[308]

In a second powerful article, published in May 2021,[309] arguing for a Palestinian refugee right of return, Beinart asks, "Why is dreaming of return laudable for Jews but pathological for Palestinians?" If one accepts that a one-state solution is the only possible outcome, it follows that there must be a Palestinian right of return. Beinart acknowledges that "Envisioning return requires uprooting deeply entrenched structures of Jewish supremacy and Palestinian subordination. It requires envisioning a different kind of country . . . It would require redistributing land, economic resources, and political power, and perhaps just as painfully, reconsidering cherished myths about the Israeli and Zionist past. At this juncture in history, it is impossible to know how so fundamental a transition might occur, or if it ever will."

The one-state solution may seem like a febrile pipe-dream that ignores reality and is impossible to achieve, but nonetheless the ground may be shifting in its favour. *The Economist*, in a May 2021 leader,[310] said, "[I]nstead of being a pathway to peace, the two-state "process" is barring the route. Everyone pretends that peace is still on the agenda when, in reality, it is not . . . [T]he new Palestinian vision is to demand individual rights in one state." The influential newspaper noted that Palestinians have become part of America's culture wars, with progressives in the Democratic Party starting to declare that

---

308 Bret Stephens, "The Siren Song of 'One State'," *The New York Times*, August 3, 2020 https://www.nytimes.com/2020/08/03/opinion/israel-palestine-one-state-solution.html (accessed July 27, 2021). Stephens and Beinart have become sparring partners. See, for example, https://www.youtube.com/watch?v=Zo-i344ir5Y

309 Peter Beinart, "Teshuvah: A Jewish Case for Palestinian Refugee Return," *Jewish Currents*, May 11, 2021 https://jewishcurrents.org/teshuvah-a-jewish-case-for-palestinian-refugee-return/ (accessed July 26, 2021).

310 "Two States or One?" *The Economist*, May 29, 2021 https://www.economist.com/leaders/2021/05/27/two-states-or-one (accessed July 26, 2021).

Palestinian lives matter, a dramatic and emotion-laden way to express the pro-Palestinian argument. Adam Serwer, a biracial Jewish staff writer at *The Atlantic*, has said "obviously support for a version of the two-state solution that is simply a fig leaf for further de facto annexation or oppression of Palestinians is not progressive . . . as an American, I do not want to live in a country where first-class citizenship is defined by race, ethnicity, or religion, so it would be absurd to demand Palestinians or anyone else accept such an arrangement elsewhere."[311]

But what about the huge demographic issue? The obvious problem with the simple one-state solution, a state stretching from the Jordan River to the Mediterranean Sea with all of its citizens having equal rights, is that immediately upon its creation there would be approximately the same number of Arabs and Jews and, in due course, likely more Arabs than Jews (particularly if there were to be a generous Palestinian right of return).[312] The simple one-state solution would eventually—perhaps immediately—put Jews in the minority. It is impossible to see the Jewish citizens of the contemporary State of Israel, and many Jews in the Diaspora, agreeing to this. Such a proposal, it seems, subverts the whole idea of Israel.

There is an answer to this problem, imperfect but plausible. In a powerful and important book, the American philosopher Omri Boehm argues for the creation of a federal, binational republic, that he calls the Haifa Republic.[313] The Haifa Republic is not a pure single state solution. It is a federation, a modified two-state solution, but with a

---

311 Adam Serwer, "The Cruelty Is the Point," *Jewish Currents*, July 29, 2021 https://mailchi.mp/262d11a88ea7/thursday-newsletter-6245423?e=7a79377d0f (accessed July 29, 2021).

312 This despite the dramatically increasing birthrate of Israeli Jews. See "In Israel, Birth Rates Are Converging Between Jews and Muslims," *The Economist*, August 18, 2022 https://www.economist.com/middle-east-and-africa/2022/08/18/in-israel-birth-rates-are-converging-between-jews-and-muslims?frsc=dg%7Ce (accessed August 20, 2022).

313 Note 288. Boehm is not alone in advancing this idea. See Jodi Rudoren, "It's Time to Talk Seriously About a Confederation of Israel and Palestine," *Forward*, June 3, 2022 https://forward.com/opinion/504687/its-time-to-talk-seriously-about-a-confederation-of-israel-and-palestine/ (accessed June 4, 2022).

crucial additional feature, a joint constitution. The Haifa Republic would recognize the right of both Jews and Palestinians to national self-determination and sovereignty in their own states, states demarcated by the so-called Green Line borders that were established de facto in 1949, and yet collectively regulate their separate sovereignty by a joint constitution ensuring human rights, freedom of movement (including across Green Line borders), and economic liberties of all. This approach to political organization is quite familiar to a Canadian living in a confederation of people with different cultures, languages, laws, and traditions—we might even call it the "Canadian Solution." Formal adoption of Green Line borders would mean that East Jerusalem, the West Bank, and Gaza Strip would be part of the new Arab state. The main issue with the Boehm proposal is whether the guarantees offered by a joint constitution would deal effectively with the enormous problem of the West Bank Jewish settlements, which would find themselves in the new Arab state. The drafting of the joint constitution, the settling of its exact contents and in particular the guarantees to be offered Jewish West Bank settlers, and the determination of how the new constitution would be ratified and implemented, would all be tortuous. A lot of heavy lifting, and much time and international assistance, would be needed. The first question is who would be charged with this monumental task.

The original Zionists, says Boehm—people like Herzl himself, Ze'ev Jabotinsky and David Ben-Gurion—"believed that the Jews had the right to exercise political self-rule, administrate autonomously their own lives, and revive Jewish culture and education. But they did not believe that this should have been done in a sovereign Jewish state: the Jews' state was envisaged as a sub-sovereign political entity existing under a multinational political sovereignty."[314] What undermined the

---

314 Note 288, p. 15. Of course, there is much criticism of Boehm's analysis. See, e.g., Ari Hoffman, "High and Low Israel Criticism," *Tablet*, June 6, 2022 https://www.tabletmag.com/sections/israel-middle-east/articles/high-and-low-israel-criticism (accessed June 19, 2022). "Boehm eagerly calls on . . . out-of-context and since-discarded ideas from the Zionist archives in support of his cause."

original Zionist agenda? The Holocaust, which destroyed the Jews' trust in a liberal democratic world order and prepared international public opinion for an ethnic Jewish state. "If pluralistic democracy could not protect Jewish life where Jews were a minority, Jews needed their own, exclusive state."[315] But Boehm rejects this approach, and distinguishes between self-determination and sovereignty, a distinction which will permit a liberal state that belongs to and protects all citizens equally, whoever they are.[316] As for the Holocaust, Boehm writes that at present Holocaust commemoration is the cornerstone of Israeli society, and the result is "an identity politics that is sponsored by the state but runs counter to the power of citizenship. It unites Jews *as opposed to* all citizens, promoting nationalism as opposed to patriotism."[317]

---

315 Note 288, pp. 16–17.
316 In 1968 Jacqueline Shohet Kahanoff suggested a Levantine model. "A modernized Levantine framework, comprising people who are different, equal, and equally native, might provide a workable—not perfect, but workable—pattern for coexistence." Note 91, p. 246. Kahanoff notes that Western nation states are being Levantinized with various types of communities being incorporated in wide and loosely organized entities.
317 Note 288, pp. 62–63.

CHAPTER 6

JEWS AS VICTIMS

Jews have been victims for so long at the hands of so many. It's undeniable. But are they still victims? Or are they now superheroes, military and economic geniuses running a hugely prosperous nuclear-armed regional superpower, worldwide leaders in business, the arts and the sciences, winners of Nobel Prizes and Academy Awards, accumulators of honours and wealth, full of power, a small group of people internationally admired and feared? And if Jews are now superheroes, do they, nonetheless, still carry within them, burned into their psyche, the stamp and burden of the eternal victim? And if they are feared and admired, are they also resented and hated because of their success? And does the stamp and burden of the eternal victim cause Jews to strike back at this resentment and hatred in irrational and disproportionate ways?

There are two competing narratives of Jews in the modern world. One is a story of weakness, passivity, and victimhood. The other is a story of strength and power. A central dilemma of modern Jewry is how to reconcile these competing narratives.

VICTIMS

Jews across the world disagree about many fundamental things. They disagree, as we have seen, about who is a Jew, on the importance of Judaism as part of Jewish identity, and on a variety of important political issues. They argue about the ethical and political justification for Israel's creation in 1948 (there are more doubters than you might think). They dispute the fate of the Palestinians who were displaced at that time, and argue about the situation of their modern descendants. There is bitter controversy about continued Israeli presence in Arab lands seized by the country during the 1967 War.

Despite rampant disagreement on many issues, and the ambiguity of Jewish identity, Jews have pulled together to become masters of national and international identity politics. They exploit opportunities to argue, powerfully and persistently, although not always convincingly, that they are oppressed, marginalized, victimized, and ignored. Victimhood has tactical and strategic advantages. And post-Holocaust generations, it can be said, use victimhood without having earned it. The French philosopher Alain Finkielkraut is a Jew born in 1949 whose father survived Auschwitz. Finkielkraut writes, "I inherited a suffering to which I had not been subjected, for without having to endure oppression, the identity of the victim was mine. I could savor an exceptional destiny while remaining completely at ease."[318] But the Finkielkraut point of view, focussing on differences between generations, does not tell the whole story. It does not give due weight to the pain experienced directly or indirectly by all world Jewry. It does not acknowledge Jews as real victims. It does not capture the tragic view of Jewish history.

How should we think about these things? In a series of provocative essays, the American writer Dara Horne describes what she considers the approach of non-Jews to Jewish victimhood.[319] Non-Jews, Horne asserts, love dead Jews, "people whose sole attribute was that they had

318 Note 4, p. 7.
319 Note 38.

111

been murdered, and whose murders served a clear purpose, which was *to teach us something.* Jews were people who, for moral and educational purposes, were supposed to be dead."[320] She decries "a tourist-industry concept, popular in places largely devoid of Jews, called "Jewish Heritage Sites."[321] She writes about readers drowning in uplifting Holocaust fiction: "Dead Jews are supposed to teach us about the beauty of the world and the wonders of redemption—otherwise, what was the point of killing them in the first place?"[322] This way of thinking, writes Horne, "is a profound affront to human dignity." She writes about "the many strange and sickening ways in which the world's affection for dead Jews shapes the present moment."[323] The point, repellent as it may seem, is that non-Jews may love dead Jews much more than they love Jews who are alive, who they may not love at all. They may even hate them without knowing exactly why.

Even the Holocaust can be turned against itself. Writes Horne: "Yes, everyone must learn about the Holocaust so as not to repeat it. But this has come to mean that anything short of the Holocaust is, well, not the Holocaust. The bar is rather high. Shooting people in a synagogue in San Diego or Pittsburgh isn't 'systemic'; it's an act of a 'lone wolf.' And it's not the Holocaust."[324] According to the Horne analysis, the Holocaust and other egregious persecution of Jews are useful to non-Jews. They are useful in two ways. They can be used as pedagogic tools. And they raise the bar and make it easier to minimize the significance of the antisemitic murder of a handful of Jews here and there.

We must reach back centuries when thinking about Jews as victims, and not just focus on the Holocaust, to comprehend the enormity of what has happened. We must, for example, think about the two great international displacements of Jews, one at the end of the 15th century

320 Note 38, p. xiv.
321 Note 38, p. 22.
322 Note 38, p. 80.
323 Note 38, p. xxi.
324 Note 38, p. 187.

when Sephardic Jews were expelled from the Iberian Peninsula and went to North Africa and the Ottoman Empire, the other at the end of the 19th century and beginning of the 20th when Ashkenazi Jews (including my own ancestors), fleeing persecution, left Eastern Europe for many countries but particularly the United States. Both of these epic migrations resulted in much suffering. Most Jews can trace their origins back to one or the other of these great displacements. The echoes of that suffering are still heard. They trickle down from one generation to the next.

MAX KARP AND SIMON DUBNOW

The huge sweep of tragic Jewish history, its magnitude in space and time, renders the pain of the Jewish people almost incomprehensible, and impossible to deny or diminish. How to grapple with it? Perhaps, to gain some understanding of this pain, one needs to consider individual cases and events. Perhaps victimhood can best be understood one Jew at a time. Grand narratives and statistical compilations are not adequate. The stories of Max Karp and Simon Dubnow may help. I chose their stories more or less at random. There are so many stories to choose from.

Mendel Max Karp was a violinist. He was born in Poland in 1892. As an adult Karp lived in Berlin, but he was deported to Poland (to a town just over the German/Polish border) on October 28, 1938, as one of 17,000 Polish nationals, almost all of them Jews, expelled at that time as part of the Nazi *Polenaktion* (the "Polish Action").[325] He was not welcome in the country of his birth. Karp managed to return to Berlin where he tried desperately to arrange passage to Shanghai where he would be safe. World War II broke out and prevented his emigration.

---

325 For Max Carp's personal account of *Polenaktion*, see "We Were Being Driven Like Hunted Animals," Jüdisches Museum Berlin https://www.jmberlin.de/en/max-karp-polenaktion (accessed December 1, 2021).

He was interned as a stateless European Jew in Sachsenhausen concentration camp, where he was murdered on January 27, 1940. Writes Götz Aly: "The German government persecuted him, deprived him of his livelihood as a musician, turned him into a door-to-door tinker, and forced him to the border. The Polish government stripped him of his citizenship and then refused to take him in."[326] A photograph of Max Karp in the collection of Berlin's Jewish Museum shows a well-dressed middle-aged man with a moustache reading a newspaper. He seems to be in a nicely furnished living room of a house or apartment. He is looking at the camera with a slight smile. The photograph was taken in Berlin about 1935.[327]

Simon Dubnow was born in 1860 in a Russian shtetl, the son of a wood seller. He became an eminent Jewish historian, writer, and activist, and is considered one of the greatest advocates of Diaspora nationalism.[328] In 1922 Dubnow left Russia for Berlin. In 1925–1929, his ten-volume *World History of the Jewish People* was published in German. In 1933, after Hitler came to power, Dubnow left Berlin and went to Riga in Latvia. But he was not safe there. When the Germans seized Riga in July 1941, Dubnow was forced into the Riga ghetto. On December 8, 1941, German soldiers murdered him as part of the infamous massacre of 25,000 Jews in the Rumbula forest near Riga. Dubnow, too old and ill to make his way to the forest despite Nazi orders to do so, was shot on the street.[329] Because of his eminence, there are a number of photographs of Dubnow, mostly taken later in his life. They show a genial-looking man of small stature, with white hair and a goatee, wire-rimmed glasses, well-dressed in a three-piece suit, wearing a watch chain—obviously a person of substance and achievement, the quintessential gentle professor and scholar.

---

326 Note 32, pp. 2–4.
327 See note 325.
328 See Saul Goodman, "Simon Dubnow-A Revaluation," *Commentary* December 1960 https://www.commentary.org/articles/saul-goodman/simon-dubnow-a-revaluation/ (accessed December 1, 2021).
329 See Aly, note 32, pp. 36–37.

FRENCH CHILDREN

Then we might ponder the stories of the French children of the Holocaust. In 1996 Serge Klarsfeld published a memorial to these children, after years of laborious and meticulous research.[330] The Klarsfeld memorial chronicles the lives of more than 11,000 French Jewish children, from Occupied and Vichy France, arrested by the Germans with the often enthusiastic help of the French state. These children were deported to German camps where all but about 300 died. Often children and parents, and siblings, were deported separately, in acts of wanton and extreme cruelty. Sometimes infants were sent to death camps by themselves with no one to look after them along the way.

Klarsfeld has assembled, from various sources, pictures of 2,500 of these children. Some of these pictures, taken perhaps in a photographer's studio, show children in formal poses, with props such as a vase of flowers or a teddy bear or a parasol or a book, the girls often with bows in their hair. Some are more like casual family snapshots, sometimes outside in a garden. Some are taken from official documents such as a *carte d'identité*. I have studied all of these photographs. In most of them, the children look happy. They are well-dressed. Some are wearing a yellow star. Some have mischievous grins. Sometimes they are with their parents and siblings, perhaps arm-in-arm. Sometimes they are alone. Some are infants. Some are babies. In most cases, Klarsfeld gives the addresses of these children and their families at the time they were arrested and deported (what does it mean to "arrest" a child?). I have looked at pictures of some of these addresses on the Internet. Somehow seeing these places as they are now, ordinary and innocent, perhaps an apartment building in a modest part of Paris, with a hairdresser or tailor at street level, only accentuates the horror of what happened decades ago. Klarsfeld's extraordinary book makes an incomprehensible

---

330 Serge Klarsfeld, *French Children of the Holocaust: A Memorial* (New York: New York University Press, 1996). This book has 1,881 pages.

tragedy accessible by its concentration on individual cases and use of photographs.

Here are a few of those cases, as documented by Klarsfeld.

Monique Adelski, a beautiful girl with long hair, and a big smile, was born on November 9, 1938, in Paris. She was deported on May 20, 1944.

Francine Beirach was four and a half years old when she was deported on August 5, 1942. Klarsfeld notes, "there is no trace of Francine on the deportation lists where her name should have been. Perhaps she was one of those very young children, alone and in anguish and unable to state their identity when deported, for whom all means of identification were lost." In her photograph, Francine holds a teddy bear (many of the children in the Klarsfeld photographs are clutching stuffed animals).

Charles Bernat was born in Paris on July 8, 1941; he was deported on September 18, 1942; he was murdered in Auschwitz three days later, upon arrival, on September 21, 1942. In his photograph, Charles is laughing.

Jacqueline Bernheim was deported on May 20, 1944, nine days after her sixth birthday—her photograph shows a beautiful girl with pigtails, holding several stuffed animals.

Liliane Lip was born on May 12, 1940, and was deported, alone, in September 1942. Her parents had been deported, separately, on earlier convoys.

Marcelle Pisanti was one year old when she was deported, with her mother and father, on June 30, 1944.

Denise Sternzus was 14 years old when she was deported on September 15, 1942. She lived in the apartment building I stayed in on Ile Saint-Louis in Paris in 2019 (see Chapter 2).

MARCEL HIMEL

Sometimes it helps, to better understand such things, to talk about someone you knew. Or almost knew. Marcel Himel was a Jewish child in Nazi-occupied France. He survived and died in Toronto on July 8, 2021, at the age of 84. His original name was Marcel Grinblatt (he was adopted by the Himel family in 1961 in Toronto). His childhood story is one of displacement, deprivation, and loss. I talked about Marcel's life with his widow, Patty Himel, and his daughter, Nicole Himel. They lent me a collection of Marcel's papers dealing with the Grinblatt family's experiences during the Nazi years.

Marcel was born on December 4, 1936, in Paris. His parents were Albert and Régine Grinblatt. In a letter I found among Marcel's papers, a friend of his mother described her as "une femme charmante, resplaudissante de beauté et de bonté."

The Grinblatt family lived in a four-room apartment at 32 Rue du Temple in Paris. In June 1942, Marcel's father, aged 33, was arrested by the Nazis at the apartment, taken to the Beaune-la-Roland Internment Camp, and deported from there on Convoy 5 which left for Auschwitz on June 28, 1942. He was murdered in Auschwitz: the exact date is not known, but is thought to be sometime shortly after he arrived. Régine and Marcel were sent to Camp Douadic, a "reception center" for Jews about 300 kilometres south of Paris. Later, Marcel and his mother somehow found their way from Douadic to Annecy in Vichy France, an area occupied at the time by Italian soldiers who were not interested in pursuing Jews and sometimes protected them. Marcel and his mother stayed at the Hôtel des Marquisats which was designated as a "centre d'accueil" for Jewish women and children.[331] Marcel, aged six, was enrolled at the local primary school, Ecole Quai Jules Philippe.

The Italians left Annecy in September 1943, and the Germans once more took control of the region. They resumed persecution of Jews.

---

331 The Hôtel des Marquisats is still in business. Its website tells us that the "hotel offers a quiet and peaceful place throughout the year."

Marcel's mother and more than 30 other Jews (the exact number is not certain) were arrested on Tuesday, November 16, 1943, in the late afternoon, at the Hôtel des Marquisats. This became known as "la Rafle [roundup] des Marquisats." Marcel, along with several other children, escaped the roundup; we don't know how. Régine Grinblatt was taken to Drancy, and then deported to Auschwitz on Convoy 62 along with other Jewish women and children arrested at the hotel. She had to pay "the expenses of her deportation"—750 francs. Régine died in Auschwitz. We don't know the date of her death.

Marcel was taken, by an unknown person, to Izieu, less than 100 kilometres from Annecy. He arrived two days after la Rafle des Marquisats, on November 18. In Izieu there was a small orphanage and school, established in May 1943, where Jewish children were hidden. Later it became known as "la Maison d'Izieu" and the children were called the "enfants d'Izieu." Marcel did not stay there for long. He may have left as early as December, although we do not know where he went or who took him in. He was not at the Maison d'Izieu when, on April 6, 1944, the Lyon Gestapo, under the command of Klaus Barbie, came in two lorries and arrested forty-four children, ranging in age from five (Albert Bulka) to seventeen (Arnold Hirsch), and seven teachers. This is known as "la Rafle d'Izieu." On April 13, thirty-four children and four teachers were deported on Convoy 71 from Drancy to Auschwitz; others followed shortly. Only one person, the teacher Léa Feldblum, survived.

It is not clear what happened to Marcel Grinblatt after he left the Maison d'Izieu. What we do know is that he arrived at Pier 21 in Halifax on September 19, 1948, unaccompanied, as a passenger on the MS Sobieski, a ship of the Gdynia-America Line. He boarded the ship by himself in Cannes. Marcel was twelve years old. Then, somehow, he made his way to Toronto where he was taken in by the Himel family and began a new life.

Among Marcel Himel's papers are photocopies of pages from a 1992 book by New York lawyer Louis Nizer.[332] The book is about Nizer's

---

332 Louis Nizer, *Catspaw* (New York: D.I. Fine, 1992).

successful defense of a Holocaust survivor called Murray Gold who was falsely accused of multiple murders. Marcel highlighted a passage about Gold: "When he arrived in the United States at the age of fifteen he had not only suffered the anguish of his flight and deep fears, he was burdened with other heavy handicaps. He knew no English. He had been reared in the language and customs of his parents. He was a child, but like many immigrants he carried the sorrows and anguish of the adults. He had been deprived of the joys and lightheartedness of childhood."[333] Other passages highlighted by Marcel refer to the emotional illness, particularly persecution trauma, that can be seen "among those who at a very early age became victims of life under Nazi rule and who have lost loved ones," including "paranoid features, querulousness, suspiciousness and fantasies."[334]

Marcel's widow and his daughter say that Marcel never spoke about his wartime experiences. They say he never lost his temper. He never swore. They say he was the gentlest of men.

SUPERHEROES

If non-Jews—some of them, anyway—think about Jewish victimhood the way Dara Horne describes it, what about Jews themselves? They think about victimhood, of course, with sadness and anger and, perhaps, resignation. Shame, as well? Is it shameful to be a passive victim, and not fight back, a highly controversial charge sometimes levelled against Jews, particularly in the context of the Holocaust? Is it shameful to tolerate what should not be tolerated? Is it shameful to placate and appease your enemies? Is it shameful to live in degrading circumstances? Is it shameful to be on the run? Is it better to fight, knowing you will die?[335]

---

333 Note 332, p. 178.
334 Note 332, p. 179.
335 For a discussion of these troubling issues, see, e.g., Michael Marrus, *The Holocaust in History* (New York: Meridian, 1987), chapter 6.

One of the great allures of Israel is that Jews are not victims in that place. The Jews of Israel control a vibrant country with a booming economy that bestrides the Middle East as a regional superpower equipped with nuclear weapons. What an achievement! Success has crowded out whatever shame there may once have been. During the June 1967 Six-Day War, I was a student in England. I remember vividly how excited and gratified I was by the extraordinary military success of Israel. I rented a tiny black-and-white television so I could sit in my room and follow the dramatic events as they unfolded. I watched Israeli tanks sweep through the desert, driving Arab armies before them. I saw troops, commanded by the buccaneering and flamboyant General Moshe Dayan in his eye-patch, capture East Jerusalem. Jews were no longer weak. They were no longer victims. They were no longer passive. They were warriors.

David Baddiel writes, "Israelis *aren't* very Jewish . . . They're too macho, too ripped and aggressive and confident."[336] Shlomo Sand has drawn attention to the way Israelis, and particularly their leaders, abandoned their old Jewish names and replaced them with Hebrew ones when Israel was created. David Green became David Ben-Gurion. Szymon Perski became Shimon Peres. And so on. Writes Sand: "The old names evoked the weak Jews who had been led to concentration camps and massacred like cattle, or those who slavishly aped Islamic civilization. The point was to create a 'new man' in Israel, a muscular Hebrew full of vigour, physical as well as spiritual."[337] The new Hebrew-speaking Jews of Israel were not weak. They were macho and ripped. Jews had a new identity.

There are consequences to the perception of Jew as superhero. Marc Tracy has argued that, when it comes to Israel, a new generation of American Jews no longer easily accepts the idea that Jews possess special obligations towards one another. "For years, American Jews could look upon Israel as a tiny state full of long-oppressed people with hostile neighbors . . ." But now, says Tracy, some American Jews "view the Mideast conflict structurally, as another instance of one powerful

336 Note 48, p. 92.
337 Note 29. pp. 49–50.

group's oppressing the less powerful one."[338] Why would you help or approve of such oppression? Why would you especially care for the welfare of a nation of superheroes dominating its neighbours? Why would you identify with these people?

The philosopher Omri Boehm has a different perspective on Jewish identity. The modern Israeli may be a new man, but he is a new man obsessed with the past. He has moved on, but carries the history of his people with him. He still embraces victimhood. Boehm adopts the approach of Yehuda Elkana, a Hungarian scientist and historian who survived Auschwitz.[339] Interpreting and quoting Elkana, Boehm writes, "Modern democratic societies are ruled by economic, social, psychological, and ideological considerations—the building blocks of a compromise born of open, rational exchange—but Israelis are motivated by 'deep existential *Angst*.' For too long, Israel's public has been governed by a 'certain interpretation of the Holocaust,' a mythical, metaphysical account of anti-Semitism according to which 'the whole world is against us,' and we are 'the eternal victim.'"[340] Furthermore, with the Holocaust the basis of national consciousness, it became easy to think that Palestinians fought Zionism "not for political causes— land, citizen rights, borders, self-determination, religious sites—but out of a metaphysical, anti-Semitic wish to exterminate the Jews."[341]

The modern Israeli, and perhaps the modern Jew, may be a superhero, but he is a superhero suffering from deep existential angst. He has the weight of a tragic history on his shoulders. He still fears that his enemy seeks nothing less than his extermination. He is both superhero and victim.

---

338 Marc Tracy, "Inside the Unraveling of American Zionism: How a New Generation of Jewish Leaders Began to Rethink Their Support for Israel," *The New York Times*, November 2, 2021 https://www.nytimes.com/2021/11/02/magazine/israel-american-jews.html (accessed November 11, 2021).

339 See Yehuda Elkhana's famous article (in Hebrew), "In Praise of Forgetting," *Haaretz*, March 2, 1988, discussed by Boehm, note 288, pp. 68–71.

340 Note 288, p. 70.

341 Note 288, p. 88.

CHAPTER 7

JEWS AND
THE MEDIA

ACQUIRING IDENTITY

How a person and a community think of themselves, and how others think of them—the identity they acquire and possess—depends on how they are depicted. There will be competing depictions. A person and a community will describe themselves, but the world will see that as self-serving and apply a big discount. What really counts is what outsiders say. At the end of the day, we do not create our own identity. Others do it for us, directly and indirectly. Our identity is thrust upon us. Alain Finkielkraut quotes Sartre: "It is sufficient that others look at me for me to be what I am."[342] Or, as the central character in Luigi Pirandello's play *Right You Are (If you think so)* puts it, "I am whoever you think I am." When it comes to describing us and our community, outsiders may be prejudiced, misinformed, and badly motivated, perhaps cynically seeking some kind of strategic advantage. And they may disagree. We

342 Note 4, p. 171.

may even disagree, among ourselves, about our identity. We may be unsure who we are. Outsiders may be more certain. It's easier for them. And more fun.

Once upon a time, starting in the 15th century, much creation and depiction of identity happened in print—books (particularly novels), pamphlets, then newspapers—and sometimes on the stage. The reach of these media, initially small, quickly became big. By 1500, in Europe, there were printing presses in more than 150 places, and probably at least 13 million books in circulation (Europe then had a population of about 100 million).[343] It is estimated that 200 million books were printed in Europe in the 16th century. This was the beginning of what Benedict Anderson calls "print-capitalism." Anderson argues that the biggest consequence of print-capitalism was the development of "national print-languages" allowing many people to read the same thing at the same time. Few more important things have happened in history. It made possible "imagined communities" leading to modern nation-states. Thus was born nationalism, a new and potent force.[344] Nationalism begat xenophobia.[345] Nationalism and xenophobia made a particular enemy of the Jews, a displaced people without a country. There was no room for Jews in somebody else's nation-state. The only solution for Jews was to become nationalists themselves and acquire their own nation-state. Zionism was the solution. Or so many Jews (not all) thought.

Print-capitalism was an enemy of Jews in another way as well. Newly developing media often depicted Jews in stereotyped, unflattering, hostile, ways, both reflecting and influencing society's attitudes. Print-capitalism made these depictions widespread and easily available. The most notorious Jew in English literature is Shylock, the money-lender in Shakespeare's *The Merchant of Venice* (circa 1597). Shylock does not

---

343 Asa Briggs and Peter Burke, *A Social History of the Media*, Fourth Edition (Cambridge: Polity Press, 2020), p. 24.
344 Anderson, note 3. See Chapter 3 in particular.
345 See George Makari, *Of Fear and Strangers: A History of Xenophobia* (New York: Norton, 2021).

stand alone as a stereotype. There is Barabbas in Christopher Marlowe's play *The Jew of Malta* (1590); the pickpocket Fagin in *Oliver Twist* by Charles Dickens (1838); Steiner in Rudyard's Kipling story *Bread Upon the Waters* (1898) (Kipling was a well-known believer in the fraudulent *Protocols of the Elders of Zion*); Anthony Trollope's Ferdinand Lopez in *The Prime Minister* (1875); I.Z. Barnett in Hilaire Belloc's *Emmanuel Burden* (1904) and subsequent Belloc novels; the financier Simon Rosedale in Edith Wharton's *House of Mirth* (1905); and Dr. Gluck in G.K. Chesterton's *The Flying Inn* (1914). The list goes on and on and on, over hundreds of years, in tens of thousands of books and plays, in many countries and languages (the examples I give are all from English literature). The nuances are few.[346]

SOCIAL MEDIA

Print capitalism has been replaced by social media capitalism. Traditional media have been crushed; they barely exist. The main means of identity construction and depiction are now social media—Facebook, Twitter, Instagram and WhatsApp (both owned by Facebook), TikTok, etc.—all with vast audiences and influence, operating globally and chaotically, transcending national languages (but, interestingly enough, not entirely subverting, sometimes reinforcing, traditional nationalism). Facebook has over three billion users, more than a third of the planet's population. *The New York Times*, arguably the world's pre-eminent English language newspaper, has by comparison a trivial circulation of about eight million, almost all for its digital edition.

Social media has replaced personal contact. Perceptions of identity come from social media posts, not from interaction with real people.

---

346 See Bryan Cheyette, *An Overwhelming Question: Jewish Stereotyping in English Fiction and Society, 1875–1914,* Thesis Presented for the Degree of Doctor of Philosophy, University of Sheffield, May 1983 https://core.ac.uk/download/pdf/9554618.pdf (accessed November 10, 2021).

Earlier (Chapter 3) I mentioned the anthropologist Aomar Boum's observation about Morocco, that older Moroccans had intimate knowledge of Jews, or received such knowledge from their parents, grandparents, and great-grandparents, while younger Moroccans have never met a Jew and get their ideas about Jews solely from media.[347] A 2021 survey in Germany found that about half of German citizens say they have never had any contact with Jews or Jewish life. "Close to one in two respondents—46 percent—said they had never had any personal contact with a Jewish person or with Jewish life more broadly, with just 16.6 percent saying that they had Jewish friends or acquaintances . . . For 55 percent of those surveyed, their perceptions of Jewish life were predominantly shaped by political and historical events. Nearly 20 percent of respondents cited the Nazi Holocaust as their frame of reference, with 14.2 percent citing the present rise of antisemitism in Germany and nearly 22 percent citing the conflict between Israel and the Palestinians. By contrast, just under 12 percent mentioned Jewish contributions to German arts and culture or science as their frame of reference."[348] A bizarre scheme called "Meet a Jew" was created in 2020 by the Central Council of Jews in Germany. It seeks to introduce Jews to non-Jewish people. The project coordinator says, "It is really important to be visible to achieve the goal of normalcy, so Jewish people aren't perceived as something unknown or foreign . . ."[349]

Social media, replacing personal contact, are used to express individual opinion, promote the opinions of others, form groups committed to a particular belief or course of action, and disseminate alleged "facts" and "information." There is little or no editorial curation

347 See note 212.
348 "Survey Showing That Nearly Half of German Citizens Have Never Had Contact with Jews Causes Worry Among Jewish Leaders," *The Algemeiner*, December 2, 2021 https://www.algemeiner.com/2021/11/22/survey-showing-that-nearly-half-of-german-citizens-have-never-had-contact-with-jews-causes-worry-among-jewish-leaders/ (accessed December 2, 2021).
349 Peter Yeung, "Meet a Jew," *Slate*, December 28, 2021 https://slate.com/human-interest/2021/12/meet-a-jew-germany-anti-semitism-crime.html (accessed January 5, 2022).

of these opinions and assertions, this despite the weak protestations of social media bosses, the invocation by them of fatuous self-invented "community guidelines," "rules," and measures to "improve the user experience," the self-righteous tut-tutting of academic and social commentators, the chest-thumping of confused politicians seeking an issue, and flailing ineffectual government hearings and attempts at regulation. In 2017 Tom Friedman of *The New York Times* described the Internet as "an open sewer of untreated, unfiltered information."[350] Friedman was right then and his description still applies. Absurd and inflammatory views, lies, and abuse appear on social media and girdle the globe in an instant, pushing opinion this way and that.

Increasingly there are pleas and plans for government to regulate or repress postings of this kind or require that this be done directly by social media platforms themselves. For example, in December 2021 a U.K. parliamentary committee recommended that social media companies "design their systems to identify, limit the spread of, and remove antisemitic material quickly after it is reported."[351] In 2022 the U.K. government introduced a broad Online Safety Bill (running to several hundred pages) that, among other things, would impose a "duty of care" on tech firms requiring them to protect their users from, for example, racism and sexual exploitation—indeed, anything that is deemed "harmful." The Canadian government has proposed similar legislation and referred the matter to an advisory panel which was unable to agree even on how to define "online harms," let alone on how to regulate them.[352]

350 Tom Friedman, "Online and Scared," *The New York Times*, January 11, 2017 https://www.nytimes.com/2017/01/11/opinion/online-and-scared.html (accessed November 8, 2021).
351 See Lee Harpin, "Social Media Firms Urged to Make 'Major Changes' to Stop Antisemitic Abuse," *Jewish News*, December 14, 2021 https://www.jewishnews.co.uk/social-media-firms-urged-to-make-major-changes-to-stop-antisemitic-abuse/ (accessed December 20, 2021). For the text of the report, see https://publications.parliament.uk/pa/jt5802/jtselect/jtonlinesafety/129/12902.htm
352 An absurd example of government regulation is 2022 legislation of the Canadian government criminalizing the "communication of statements, other than in

We should be highly cautious about proposals like these. It is a bad idea to try and censor what some regard as wrong or offensive posts on social media, or ban allegedly egregious individuals or organizations from participating in these platforms. Censorship by government is particularly dangerous, easily used by unscrupulous leaders in pursuit of an unsavoury agenda. The price of freedom of expression, for being able to express your own views, is allowing a platform for the views of others, views that you may consider threatening, untrue, or repellent. After all, these other people may regard your views the same way as you regard theirs. The correct response to misinformation is to give facts; the correct reply to a bad argument is a good argument. There are very few justifiable exceptions to freedom of expression on social media. (One is the regulation of bot networks generating mass automatic posts.[353] The aim of such bots is often to subvert free and democratic societies by, for example, tricking voters during an election.)

What if the social media depiction of Jews, the Jewish community, or Jewish affairs is dangerous, untrue, or repellent? Is that a special case, like bot networks, demanding regulation? In the face of antisemitism, what should prevail, pleas for stringent regulation or appeals for freedom of expression? It helps to consider the kind of antisemitism we are talking about. Most social media antisemitism has lack of civility as its essence. Civility in society is highly desirable, but not essential. Incivility is unpleasant, but seldom dangerous, and will always be with us. Civility should not be enforced at the expense of freedom of expression. It is not the purpose of law to enforce civility; that is a job for civil society, using social pressure. Although, in some circumstances, lack of civility

private conversation, that wilfully promote anti-Semitism by condoning, denying or downplaying the Holocaust." This new crime can be found in Section 319 of the Canadian Criminal Code. What was in the mind of those who promoted such a pointless limitation of freedom of expression?

353 See, e.g., Muyi Xiao, Paul Mozur, and Gray Beltran, "Buying Influence: How China Manipulates Facebook and Twitter," *The New York Times*, December 20, 2021 https://www.nytimes.com/interactive/2021/12/20/technology/china-facebook-twitter-influence-manipulation.html?referringSource=articleShare (accessed December 20, 2021).

can incite violence, even mass violence. Then the calculus is different. Freedom of expression does not permit incitement to violence.

MOBS AND LIES

Antisemitic lies and abuse are everywhere and are given huge velocity by media mobs. After the shooting at the Tree of Life Synagogue in Pittsburgh, on October 27, 2018, when eleven worshippers were killed and six wounded, a large number of antisemitic images and videos were quickly uploaded onto Instagram. *The New York Times* made a social media search immediately following the shooting for postings made after the event. The paper reported: "A search for the word "Jews" displayed 11,696 posts with the hashtag "#jewsdid911," claiming that Jews had orchestrated the September 11 terror attacks. Other hashtags on Instagram referenced Nazi ideology, including the number 88, an abbreviation used for the Nazi salute 'Heil Hitler.'"[354] One day after the shooting a new video added to Instagram "claimed that the state of Israel was created by the Rothschilds, a wealthy Jewish family. Underneath the video, the hashtags read #conspiracy and #jewworldorder. By late Monday, it had been viewed more than 1,640 times and shared to other social media sites, including Twitter and Facebook." Social media companies, said the newspaper, "cannot put the genie back in the bottle" and cannot police disinformation and hate speech.

There is no reason to think that the situation has improved since October 2018. For example, social media were rife with misinformation and prejudice, on both sides of the conflict, during the May 2021 confrontation between Israel and Palestinians centering on the Gaza Strip. *The New York Times* reported, "The false information has included

---

354 Sheera Frenkel, Mike Isaac and Kate Conger, "On Instagram, 11,696 Examples of How Hate Thrives on Social Media," *The New York Times*, October 29, 2018 https://www.nytimes.com/2018/10/29/technology/hate-on-social-media.html (accessed November 5, 2021).

videos, photos and clips of text purported to be from government officials in the region, with posts baselessly claiming early this week that Israeli soldiers had invaded Gaza, or that Palestinian mobs were about to rampage through sleepy Israeli suburbs. The lies have been amplified as they have been shared thousands of times on Twitter and Facebook, spreading to WhatsApp and Telegram groups . . ."[355] A few days later, the newspaper reported on a surge of provocative activity by Jewish extremists on WhatsApp. A number of WhatsApp and Telegram groups were formed for the purposes of instigating and committing violence against Palestinians.[356] A January 2022 report by the Israeli Diaspora Affairs Ministry found a 1,200 per cent hike in antisemitic posts on social media platforms (mostly on Twitter) during May 2021.[357]

A 2020 large-scale quantitative study of online antisemitism[358] analyzes the "weaponization" of information, primarily by nationalistic and racist alt-right groups. More than 100 million social media posts and seven million posted images were analyzed. The study found "evidence of increasing antisemitism and the use of racially charged language, in large part correlating with real-world political events like the 2016 US Presidential Election."[359] It concluded: "The present work provides solid quantified evidence that the technology . . . is being

355 Sheera Frenkel, "Lies on Social Media Inflame Israeli-Palestinian Conflict," *The New York Times*, May 14, 2021 https://www.nytimes.com/2021/05/14/technology/israel-palestine-misinformation-lies-social-media.html (accessed October 14, 2021).

356 Sheera Frankel, "Mob Violence Against Palestinians in Israel Is Fueled by Groups on WhatsApp," *The New York Times*, May 19, 2021 https://www.nytimes.com/2021/05/19/technology/israeli-clashes-pro-violence-groups-whatsapp.html (accessed October 15, 2021).

357 "Violent Antisemitism Spiked on Social Media During Gaza Operation," *The Jerusalem Post*, January 22, 2022 https://www.jpost.com/diaspora/antisemitism/article-694209 (accessed January 24, 2022).

358 Savvas Zannettou, Joel Finkelstein, Barry Bradlyn, and Jeremy Blackburn, "A Quantitative Approach to Understanding Online Antisemitism," Proceedings of the Fourteenth International AAAI Conference on Web and Social Media (ICWSM 2020), p. 786.

359 Note 358, p. 795.

co-opted by actors that have harnessed it in worrying ways, using the same concepts of scale, speed, and network effects to greatly expand their influence and effects on the rest of the Web and the world at large."[360] It seems unnecessary to conduct large-scale quantitative research to know this to be true.

An October 2021 U.K. study[361] looked at antisemitism across nine social media platforms, including Facebook, TikTok, Twitter, and YouTube. It found, for example, that content posted with the hashtags #rothschildfamily, #synagogueofsatan, and #soros was viewed 25.1 million times in half a year. The study reported: "On Facebook there are all forms of hostility towards Jews, from religiously based anti-Judaism, racist antisemitism, anti-modern antisemitism (which alleges that Jews are promoting 'modern' ideas like equality, democracy, liberalism or feminism), post-Holocaust antisemitism (that is antisemitism referring to the Holocaust, like Holocaust denial, or claiming that Jews today take advantage of the Holocaust and such), to Israel-related antisemitism. Motifs of classical anti-Judaism remain central: Jews as foreigners, as usurers and money men, as vengeful and power-seeking people, as murderers, ritual and blood cult practitioners, land robbers, destroyers and conspirators. However, the most widespread form of antisemitism online is Israel-related antisemitism, which in studies accounts for around 33.35% of total widespread antisemitism."[362] This and other forms of antisemitic comment, much of it absurd and not worth a response, exist despite the feeble attempts of Facebook to toughen enforcement of its "community standards," for example, by "deplatforming" those who do not reflect these standards, and by prohibiting Holocaust denial. The U.K. study had similar findings for

---

360 Note 358, p. 796.
361 Hope Not Hate, Amadeu Antonio Foundation, Expo Foundation, *Antisemitism in the Digital Age: Online Antisemitic Hate, Holocaust Denial, Conspiracy Ideologies and Terrorism in Europe*, October 2021 https://hopenothate.org.uk/wp-content/uploads/2021/10/google-report-2021-10-v21Oct.pdf (accessed November 4, 2021).
362 Note 361, p. 39.

other social media sites. Its report on Twitter, for example, found that "Twitter saw an upsurge in antisemitism framed as hostility towards Israel and Zionism during the May 2021 outbreak of violence in the region. While much of the antisemitism posted in this period was coded by the use of terms like 'Zionist', some took on more extreme and explicit framing. The Anti-Defamation League reported that more than 17,000 tweets containing variations of the phrase 'Hitler was right' were posted between 7-14 May . . ."[363] As for YouTube: "In August, 2021, an NGO, Center for Countering Digital Hate, published findings showing that it had identified, during a six-week period, 52 examples of content with 'clear, grotesque antisemitism' hosted on YouTube with an estimated total of more than 3,670,000 impressions, including five videos with over 800,000 views that deny aspects of the Holocaust or claim that Jews started World War II."[364]

Personal abuse of individual Jews is everywhere on social media. Here's one of innumerable examples. In Chapter 2, I mentioned the 2016 report of the U.K. House of Commons Home Affairs Committee on antisemitism in the United Kingdom.[365] A "key fact" of the report was this anecdote: "At one point during 2014, police informed the Labour MP Luciana Berger that she had received over 2,500 abusive tweets in just three days, all using the hashtag 'filthyjewbitch'."[366] Apparently a U.S.-based neo-Nazi website was responsible for many of these tweets. The U.K. report details many other antisemitic tweets directed against individual parliamentarians and others.

363 Note 361, pp. 67–68.
364 Note 361, p. 69.
365 *Antisemitism in the UK* (London: House of Commons, 2016) https://publications. parliament.uk/pa/cm201617/cmselect/cmhaff/136/136.pdf (accessed December 27, 2020).
366 Note 365, p. 3.

DISTURBING THE PEACE OF MANKIND

Every new form of media gives rise to a catastrophic narrative which shoves its benefits into the shadows. Asa Briggs and Peter Burke have written about the reaction in the 15th century to the invention of printing presses using moveable type. "Scribes, whose business was threatened by the new technology, deplored the arrival of the press . . . For churchmen, the basic problem was that print allowed readers who had a low position in the social and cultural hierarchy to study religious texts for themselves, rather than relying on what the authorities told them. For governments, the consequences of print [the spread of information] . . . were no reason for celebration." Briggs and Burke quote the 17th-century English poet Andrew Marvell: "O Printing! How thou hast disturbed the peace of Mankind!"[367]

Now the peace of Mankind is being disturbed digitally. But the horrible consequences and disturbing implications of the rise and dominance of social media—which are real enough—should not obscure social media's benefits. Many people now have a voice and influence that they were denied before. Some argue that social-media inspired "democratization of justice" has empowered the people and reduced the power of the elites, and that this is a good thing. In an earlier book I attacked this argument on the grounds that, when it came to this new form of communication, the bad outweighs the good.[368] I argued that democratization of justice is not all that it is cracked up to be. The problem, of course, as happens in a democracy, is that *all* people have been empowered, all of Jean-Paul Sartre's mediocre men, including antisemites, antivaxxers, QAnon conspiracy believers, flat-earthers, and haters of all stripes. Nonetheless, those who were once voiceless in face of the elite, an elite that relentlessly promoted views that were in its own interest, now have a voice. This is a good thing.

---

367 Briggs and Burke, note 343, p.26.
368 Philip Slayton, *Nothing Left to Lose: An Impolite Report on the State of Freedom in Canada* (Toronto: Sutherland House, 2020), chapter 5.

CODA: HEAD BUTTING

While I was writing this book I put in place a number of Google Alerts, for such words and phrases as "antisemitism," "Palestine," "Zionism," "jews + Christianity," "jews + muslims," etc. The alerts were set for 9 a.m. every morning. The result was a large daily dump into my inbox of links to bias and bile, leavened liberally with links to platitudes (e.g., "Pope Condemns Antisemitism"), and—in all fairness—some occasional interesting references. For months, every morning, I wearily studied these Google Alert results. For the most part, it was all pretty predictable and repetitious. News outlets that covered "matters of Jewish interest" would breathlessly report on any and all antisemitic incidents around the world, sometimes big but mostly small, for example: "'Holocaust was a scam' projected on Swedish shul during antisemitism conference" (*Jewish News*); "Cobb County, Georgia Passes Resolution Denouncing Antisemitism After Swastika Incidents" (*The Algemeiner*); "Palestinian woman arrested while approaching settlement armed with a knife" (*The Times of Israel*); "Germany: Neo-Nazi's ashes buried in Jewish musician's plot" (*Israel Hayom*); and "Palestinian terror groups praise deadly West Bank attack" (*The Times of Israel*). These same outlets would give opinions on every nuance of antisemitism and every perceived aggression, micro and macro, directed against Israel or Jews. Arab-oriented news organizations had, of course, the exactly opposite approach: "Zionist forces invade West Bank" (*Mehr News Agency*); "Hamas Official: Resistance best option to liberate Palestine" (*AhlulBayt News Agency*); "South Africans in Israel: A home from home for white colonialists" (*Middle East Eye*); "Zionist settler runs over two Palestinians with car in WB (*Mehr News Agency*); "Zionists Start Building Metal Structure Overlooking Al-Aqsa Mosque" (*International Quran News Agency*); "Jewish extremists provoke Muslims arriving at Jerusalem's Al-Aqsa Mosque for worship" (*Palestinian News & Information Agency*); and "Israeli Forces Open Fire at Palestinian Fishermen, Farmers in Gaza" (*Palestine Chronicle*).

CHAPTER 8

JEWS AS WANDERERS

THAT BAD DREAM

Legend says a Jew who taunted Jesus on the way to the Crucifixion was punished by being condemned to walk the Earth until the Second Coming. This unfortunate person became the Wandering Jew, a metaphorical figure who has been on the move ever since the day he was first cursed on the Via Dolorosa. Real Jews have wandered the Earth— going East, going West, going North, going South—for centuries.[369] They have been eternal refugees. Their suitcases have always been half-packed. They have constantly yearned for and sought a true home, so often denied them. To be denied a home, what for all individuals and

---

369 But Lynn Julius has written: "People in the West tend to apply a common misconception to all Jews, borrowing the European Christian notion that Jews have been guests, wandering from land to land throughout history, with no country to call their own. It is a misunderstanding: not only have Jews always lived in the patch of land in the Mediterranean which the Romans named Palestine, they have had an unbroken presence in the Middle East and North Africa for over 2,000 years . . ." See Lyn Julius, note 92, p. 6.

all peoples is central to their self-definition, existence, security, and comfort, is a bitter experience. No idea has more emotional impact and incorporates more basic human desires than the idea of home. Nothing is more destructive of the spirit than not to have a home, to have to be ready at a moment's notice to abandon the familiar, study the map, check the train schedules, and pack your bags.

Sometimes Jews have been formally expelled from countries that they considered home—their expulsion from Spain and Portugal at the end of the 15th century is a notable example. The Jews expelled from Spain and Portugal, for the most part, made their way to North Africa and the Ottoman Empire (and their descendants, hundreds of years later, to Israel, France, Canada, and other countries). Sometimes Jews were not formally expelled but might just as well have been; they fled to escape severe discrimination and persecution by the state, or by their neighbours, or by both. The Jews who fled Eastern Europe at the end of the 19th century and beginning of the 20th century are an example (my own ancestors were part of this, following a well-beaten path, Russia to Germany via Romania, Germany to France, France to England . . .). Another example is German Jews of the Nazi period who left Germany in the 1930s when the state was still aggressively encouraging Jewish emigration, before it decided, in 1941, to replace emigration with extermination. (Three hundred thousand Jews emigrated from Germany between 1933 and 1941. They found it difficult to find a country that would take them in.) Sometimes Jews left where they were living to escape poverty and seek prosperity in a new and beckoning land; much emigration to the United States was so motivated, at least in part. Sometimes they simply wished to be fully fledged first-class citizens in their own new country, rather than second-class residents in what they saw as someone else's land; the Sephardic Jews who left northern African countries for Israel after 1948, no longer willing to be *dhimmi* in Arab countries, might fit into this category. Sometimes Jews on the move were simply pursuing a dream, the dream of their own state, the dream of Israel. Sometimes, although they were well-established, perhaps even assimilated (or so they thought), in a democratic and liberal state which seemed to offer freedom and security—France, say, or England—Jews sensed a developing antisemitism, rightly or wrongly (often wrongly), and got it in their head that they should move to another country. Sometimes Jews just had to run for their lives. Mihail Sebastian, the Jewish Romanian novelist of the 1930s, wrote, "That bad dream: that suitcase packed for the journey."[370]

DUST-GRAY LAYER OF SUFFERING

Joseph Roth, an Austrian, was a friend of Stefan Zweig. In his 1927 book *The Wandering Jews*,[371] Roth writes of the early 20th-century Eastern European Jewish experience and destiny: "Eastern Jews have no home anywhere, but their graves may be found in every cemetery."[372] The Eastern Jew, writes Roth, "deep within his blood has the knowledge that he might have to flee at any moment . . . Where can he run to, if something happens? He's been on the run for thousands of years."[373] Where did Eastern Jews run to in the days of Joseph Roth? Like my grandparents, they ran to the ghettos of the West, to Vienna, Berlin, France, or America. "They gave themselves up. They lost themselves. They shed their aura of sad beauty. Instead a dust-gray layer of suffering without meaning and anxiety without tragedy settled on their stooped backs."[374]

In Vienna, writes Roth, Jews who had come from the East lived in Leopoldstadt. There is no harder lot, Roth says, than the lot of an Eastern Jew newly arrived in Vienna. The Leopoldstadt is a poor district. "There are tiny apartments that house families of six. There are

---

370 Note 95.
371 Joseph Roth, *The Wandering Jews* (New York: Norton, 2001), translation by Michael Hofmann. Originally published as *Juden auf Wanderschaft* in 1927. Roth published a new edition in 1937.
372 Note 371, p. 11.
373 Note 371, p. 98.
374 Note 371, p. 14.

tiny hostels where fifty or sixty bed down on the floors."[375] Eastern Jews needing to flee, and considering Vienna as a destination, might ask: Should we go to Berlin instead? Roth's answer: "No Eastern Jew goes to Berlin voluntarily. Who in the world goes to Berlin voluntarily?"[376] My grandparents went to Berlin voluntarily, a stop on their journey across Europe. When they lived in Berlin, perhaps my grandparents lived on the Hirtenstrasse with the other Eastern Jews. Roth calls the Hirtenstrasse the saddest street in the world. "The Hirtenstrasse is drab like a slum . . . It has a new, cheap, already-used-up, bargain-basement quality . . ."[377] After a while my grandparents left Berlin and went to Paris, in Roth's judgment a far better place for a Jew to be. "In Paris crude anti-Semitism is confined to the joyless, to the royalists, the group around *Action française* . . . Eastern Jews, accustomed to a far stronger, cruder, more brutal anti-Semitism, are perfectly happy with the French version of it."[378] (Roth wrote this only about 30 years after the Dreyfus case.) Some Jews went to America. "America signifies distance. America signifies freedom. There is always some relative or other living in America."[379] There is always a relative living in America. My father's younger brother, the second son of my grandparents, went to America from England after World War II and married Corky Hale, a well-known cabaret singer who toured with Tony Bennett and performed at the White House. The marriage didn't last long.[380]

In 1937, Joseph Roth wrote a preface to a new edition of his book. Needless to say, the circumstances of European Jews, particularly those

375 Note 371, p. 56.
376 Note 371, p. 68. In the modern day, Berlin is still not a place that welcomes refugees, particularly those from Africa, although many desperately seek entry. For a powerful fictional account of this, see Jenny Erpenbeck, *Go, Went, Gone* (New York: New Directions, 2017).
377 Note 371, p. 72.
378 Note 371, pp. 82–83. *Action française*, which still exists today, is a French far-right monarchist political movement.
379 Note 371, p. 93.
380 See Jerry Leichtling and Arlene Sarner, *Corky Hale Uncorked!: A Life of Music, Marriage, and Making a Difference* (Corky Hale Publishing, 2018).

living in Germany, were now very different. German Jews wandered still, wrote Roth, but in a different way. They mostly wandered inwardly, in their minds and souls. Roth eloquently describes their plight as the horror descended: "They wander away from friends, from familiar greetings, from kind words. They shut their eyes to deny what has just happened, which is to wander into a self-willed illusion of night. They wander away from the shock they have just experienced, into fear, which is the older sister of shock, and try to feel comfortable and at ease with fear. They wander into deception, and the worst kind of deception at that—self-deception . . . They stay, and at the same time they wander: It's a kind of contortionism of which only the most desperate prisoners are capable."[381]

ARE WE NEARLY THERE?

In her book *The Suitcase: Six Attempts to Cross a Border*,[382] Frances Stonor Saunders tells the story of a family, her family, constantly on the move, starting in the 1940s. She describes the heavy price paid for dislocation and rootlessness and failure to find a true home. Her family had Jewish antecedents, and some family members disappeared during the Nazi period, but Jewishness is largely peripheral to a story of wandering and suffering that transcends particular identities.

Saunders' grandparents, Joseph and Elena Slomnicki, both naturalized British subjects (it is unclear how this naturalization came about), were living in Romania when war broke out in 1939. Joseph was a Jew of Polish–Russian origin. Elena was not Jewish. Joseph's family was from the small town of Slomniki in Poland. In 1942, the Jews of Slomniki, more than a thousand of them, about a quarter of the town's population, were either executed in the town (the sick, the old,

---

381 Note 371, pp. 129–30.
382 Frances Stonor Saunders, *The Suitcase: Six Attempts to Cross a Border* (London: Jonathan Cape, 2021).

children) or were sent to Belzec extermination camp to be murdered there (the Jews of Lviv were also sent to Belzec—see Chapter 2).

On October 15, 1940, the Slomnicki family, along with other British subjects, were evacuated from Romania by ship. Donald Slomnicki, Frances' father, was almost ten years old (he had a younger brother, Peter). Her father's journey, writes Saunders, "in some sense . . . lasted for the rest of his life. It carried him away from his childhood, away from his father, away from the longitudes and latitudes, the guiding coordinates of his existence up to this point. He soon grew out of asking 'How long will it take?', 'Are we nearly there yet?', 'How long will we be staying here?' He learned that everything was temporary, that home was a 'for now' place, the place where your suitcase was . . ."[383]

From Romania, the family went to Istanbul. They stayed there for some weeks, before going to Cairo by train. In Cairo, Joe joined the British army, and Donald and Peter went to school. In 1942, with the Germans threatening Cairo, Elena (now called Helen) and her two sons went to South Africa (at the time Joe was stationed in Iran). After a year in South Africa, they returned to Cairo. At the end of 1944, Helen, Donald, and Peter finally reached Britain. Joe joined them later. In 1946, Joe and Helen returned to Romania, leaving their two sons in boarding school. By the end of 1948, they were back in London.

The story of this family, like the stories of so many others, is a story of dingy rented apartments, fractured relationships, dashed hopes, worry, sadness, and fear. Writes Saunders, "I have immersed myself in a story where departures lead to arrivals that are only ever the beginning of another departure; everything is transitional, there is no still point, because everything that matters—home, belonging, security—is always further away."[384]

383 Note 382 p. 131.
384 Note 382, p. 156.

SOME APPALLING GRIEF

W.G. Sebald's *The Emigrants*,[385] the stories of four people, is officially fiction, but the four people he describes are drawn from real life and their stories are largely true.[386] Each of the four is a tragic figure whose suffering has been created by travel, displacement, and loss.

Dr. Henry Selwyn, originally Hersch Seweryn, in 1899, at the age of seven, left his Lithuanian village and sailed from Riga to London. He became a surgeon. He committed suicide when an old man.

Paul Bereyter was a primary school teacher in Germany. One of his grandparents was Jewish. In 1935, just as he began his teaching career, he was given notice that he could no longer be a teacher because of his Jewish background. Shortly afterwards, his Jewish girlfriend was deported to Theresienstadt concentration camp. His father died in 1936 "from the fury and fear that had been consuming him ever since, precisely two years before his death, the Jewish families, resident in his home town of Gunzenhausen for generations, had been the target of violent attacks."[387] Paul committed suicide in 1983.

Ambrose Adelwarth, a great traveller in his early days, later "gives the impression of being filled with some appalling grief"[388] and has a "longing for an extinction as total and irreversible as possible of his capacity to think and remember."[389] Adelwarth died in a psychiatric institution in Ithaca, New York.

Max Ferber was a Jewish artist. In May 1939, aged fifteen, he left Munich and went to England by himself. In November 1941 his parents, after suffering a variety of indignities and deprivations, unable to emigrate, were deported from Munich to Riga where they were murdered by the Nazis. Ferber laments: "[T]ragedy in my youth struck

---

385 (New York: New Directions, 1997). First published as *Die Ausgewanderten* in 1992.
386 Sebald's "appropriation" of other people's stories has been criticized and resented, particularly by the people in question and their relatives.
387 Note 385, p. 53.
388 Note 385, p. 111.
389 Note 385, p. 114.

such deep roots within me that it later shot up again, put forth evil flowers, and spread the poisonous canopy over me which has kept me so much in the shade and dark . . ."[390]

In a 1997 interview about *The Emigrants*, Sebald commented: "What particularly interested me, as I began to think about these lives, was the time delay between a vicariously experienced catastrophe and the point at which it overtook these people, very late in life, i.e., the phenomenon of old age, suicide, and the way in which these kinds of drastic decisions are triggered by things that lie way back in time."[391]

THE POISONOUS CANOPY

As Sebald says, what happens early on, in the life of a person, or in the life of a people, can never be completely escaped. The highlighted photocopies found in Marcel Himel's papers (Chapter 6) suggest he never escaped the anguish of his childhood. You would expect nothing else. Donald Slomnicki, according to his daughter, never finished the journey he began when he was ten years old. Tragedy in Max Ferber's youth put forth evil flowers many years later. As for the Jewish people, the legacy of wandering hangs over them like a poisonous canopy, the way childhood events hung over the lives of Marcel, Donald, and Max.

HIER IST KEIN WARUM

Why have Jews suffered so much? Why has such an ill-defined, diverse, and disputatious community, without a common language, scattered to the four winds, for the most part not embracing a common religion,

---

390 Note 385, p. 191.
391 James Wood, "An Interview With W.G. Sebald," *Brick 59*, April 20, 2017 https://brickmag.com/an-interview-with-w-g-sebald/ (accessed December 12, 2021).

with little common ancestry and culture, been the precise target of intense and focussed prejudice and persecution for hundreds of years?

Primo Levi, the Italian-Jewish scientist and writer, was imprisoned in Auschwitz in 1944. One day, shortly after his arrival, tortured by thirst, Levi broke off an icicle outside the window of his barracks intending to lick it. A guard snatched the icicle away. "Why?" asked a desperate Levi. "Here there is no why [Hier ist kein warum]," the guard replied.

When Auschwitz was liberated, Levi was "overwhelmed by a new and vaster suffering, which had been buried and relegated to the margins of consciousness by other, more urgent sufferings: the pain of exile, of my distant home, of solitude, of lost friends, of lost youth, and of the multitude of corpses all around." He committed suicide in 1987.[392]

---

392 See Primo Levi's memoir, *If This Is a Man* (New York: The Orion Press, 1959). The memoir was originally published in 1947.

CHAPTER 9

CONCLUSION

A NEW APPROACH TO ANTISEMITISM

I have argued that the Jewish community routinely overreacts to trivial, often risible, antisemitism and harms itself in the process. To treat every antisemitic attack as equally serious is to undermine the concept of antisemitism and devalue the response to all antisemitic attacks. How does one respond sensibly, with a straight face, to allegations that Jews created the coronavirus as part of a bid for global domination, or that space lasers operated by Jews are the cause of California wild fires, or that Jews are masterminding the promotion of immigration and multiculturalism in order to replace non-Jews as rulers of society, or that Jews have secret knowledge which enables them to dominate world banking and Hollywood? I also noted earlier the inadequacy of the most widely accepted modern definition of antisemitism, the 2016 International Holocaust Remembrance Alliance (IHRA) "working definition."

We need a different and better way of thinking about and responding to antisemitism, a way that is clear and precise, calibrated, and promotes understanding and peace, rather than one that is sloppy and encourages unnecessary and dangerous conflict. We need an approach that focusses on well-defined types of antisemitic expression and their provenance, rather than one that willy-nilly emphasizes pathological motivation and wastes time decrying content that should not be taken seriously.

I suggest an approach based on identifying four types of antisemitic expression of escalating significance and concern. Each may involve word, visual image, and deed. Each calls for an appropriate and proportionate response.

The most common type of antisemitism is what I call degradation antisemitism. The concept of degradation was developed by the postcolonial theorist Homi Bhabha.[393] Bhabha says, "*Degradation* deals in images; it deals in the language of abuse; it deals in incivility." Degradation antisemitism encompasses private, individual, irrational, often thoughtless and sometimes spontaneous, non-violent but aggressive acts—for example, yelling insults on the street ("Dirty Jew!"), or daubing insulting graffiti on a wall, or uttering intemperate criticism, or publishing and distributing antisemitic literature, or denying the Holocaust.

Degradation antisemitism is not physically dangerous, although it takes an emotional toll on the victims and can lead to physical confrontation. It is generally direct and explicit, but may be indirect or coded. Accounts of degradation antisemitism, and the exaggerated cries of outrage by editorialists and citizens they inevitably occasion, are familiar to any consumer of mass media. David Baddiel argues that the rise of identity politics has changed the rules: "We live in a culture now where impact is more important than intent; where how things are taken is more significant than how they are meant."[394] Often cries of outrage serve no purpose, but they do encourage hysteria. This

---

393 See Rebecca Liu, "Why We Need a New Emotive Language of Human Rights," *Prospect*, November 5, 2019 https://www.prospectmagazine.co.uk/arts-and-books/homi-k-bhabha-interview-degradation-populism-immigration-postcolonialism-ica (accessed March 23, 2021).

394 Note 48, p. 39.

is not to minimize the cumulative effect of rampant, concerted, and organized degradation antisemitism, turbocharged by social media, and its potential to incite violence. Daniel Goldhagen has described the role and effect of officially sanctioned verbal assault on Jews in Nazi Germany, and the way in which it contributed to the "social death" of Jews and neutralized them as a factor in German life.[395]

The second type of antisemitic expression is violent antisemitism. Violent antisemitism encompasses egregious, often horrific, private acts of violence by an individual or group, sometimes spontaneous, sometimes planned, for example, in France, notoriously, the 2006 torture and murder of Ilan Halimi by about twenty young people,[396] and the 2018 murder of Mireille Knoll, an eighty-five-year-old Holocaust survivor, by two men.[397] Sometimes, at first glance, the violence may not seem to be directed at Jews specifically, for example, the January 2022 taking of hostages in a Texas synagogue by a gunman trying to secure the release of a jailed terrorist, but a closer reading of the incident will show it to be deeply antisemitic. Violent antisemitism is a matter for the state and calls for aggressive even-handed enforcement of the criminal law, which in turn requires fair and comprehensive laws, an uncorrupted and effective police force, and a strong and independent judiciary. These conditions do not always exist.

---

395 Note 31, pp. 135–7.

396 For a horrifying description of this barbaric crime, see Craig S. Smith, "Torture and Death of Jew Deepen Fears in France," *The New York Times*, March 5, 2006 https://www.nytimes.com/2006/03/05/world/europe/torture-and-death-of-jew-deepen-fears-in-france.html (accessed March 5, 2021). "[T]he case seems to embody the social problems of immigration, race and class that France has been facing with so much uncertainty. The emerging details raise deep fears of virulent anti-Semitism within the hardening underclass, and point to the decaying social fabric in which that underclass lives."

397 See "Two Men to Stand Trial in France for Killing of Jewish woman, 85," *The Guardian*, July 13, 2020 https://www.theguardian.com/world/2020/jul/13/two-men-to-stand-trial-in-france-for-killing-of-jewish-woman-85 (accessed March 5, 2021). In November 2021, one of the two men was convicted of murder and sentenced to life imprisonment, and the other was found guilty of robbery and was sentenced to fifteen years in prison.

The third type of antisemitic expression is organized private antisemitism. This is systematic discrimination, explicit or implicit, by private institutions, for example, a corporation in its hiring or promotion practices, or a club in its membership criteria, or a university in its admissions or hiring policies, or a newspaper in its routine editorial stance. Organized antisemitism should be vigorously opposed by civil society, or be made illegal, according to its nature. It requires a public policy response.

The fourth type of antisemitism expression is organized public antisemitism. This is systematic discrimination, explicit or implicit, in official government policy, laws and regulations, including the policies of major political parties (including those in opposition), often building on and embracing degradation antisemitism and inciting violent antisemitism (as in Nazi Germany). Institutional antisemitism must be attacked politically, by all citizens, using all tools available including civil disobedience, no matter the risk. It is a matter of private conscience and public duty.

The responses to expressions of antisemitism are common across countries. Cases of degradation antisemitism and violent antisemitism are typically met with outrage by Jewish groups and editorial writers and condemnation by government officials.[398] In the case of violent antisemitism, law enforcement is also engaged, sometimes energetically, sometimes without enthusiasm. Studies and surveys by Jewish groups and government committees are a typical reaction to organized private antisemitism, leading to portentous reports and sometimes reform of laws and regulations, depending upon the public policy appetite for

---

398 David Baddiel argues that "absences" are also a form of antisemitism—absences of the concern, protectiveness, and championing that other minority groups enjoy. Jews, says Baddiel, are left off the list of people we should worry about. He writes, "The problem is Jews occupy a socio-cultural grey area. Jews, although marginal, are not thought of as marginalised." The consequence is that Jews are left out when marginalised experiences are shifted into the mainstream. See Note 48, p. 37. Baddiel is obsessed with analyzing posts on Twitter. He mistakenly regards antisemitism as a form of racism when, as we have seen, Judaism is no longer thought of as being founded in race.

change. The same generally applies to organized public antisemitism, although the more pervasive and repressive this is, the less likely it is that there will be any change; to attack organized public antisemitism takes fortitude and courage.

Violent antisemitism, organized private antisemitism, and organized public antisemitism can never be ignored or justified. Degradation antisemitism, the most common type of discrimination in today's world, should generally be given little or no weight; in many cases it can be ignored. This advice may be hard to accept. The difficulty is that even the most trivial expression of degradation antisemitism, in the most benign of communities, can be fraught. That is because you don't know what it might signify or presage. History shows that it is unwise for Jews, and not just Jews, to assume their safety, even in what seems to be the most secure of circumstances. Stefan Zweig has written: "It is an iron law of history that those who will be caught up in the great movements determining the course of their own times always fail to recognise them in their early stages."[399] In the early stages of Hitler's reign as Chancellor of Germany, Zweig was living in Salzburg, not far from the Austrian–German border. "The Viennese who frequented the cafés . . . thought of National Socialism as something that was going on 'over there', and couldn't have anything to do with Austria."[400] Nonetheless, in everyone's interests, the response to degradation antisemitism should be restrained. Alain Finkielkraut has written, in his usual provocative way, that after the Holocaust, "Any reticence soon evokes the camps: the most coded expressions of anti-Semitism are immediately seen by their victims as a *will to extermination* . . . Jews have chosen stupidity and memory. They've become elephants. Inept at making distinctions, they deliberately lack subtlety and nuance. They lump finely wrought phrases together with mudslinging insults: 'your people,' uttered without any conscious malice, and the cruel and vulgar 'Dirty Jew!' are treated as if one and the same. From harmless stereotype

399 Note 27, p. 383.
400 Note 27, p. 402.

to assault to synagogue desecration, Jews flatten out every offense until it fits a single model: Auschwitz. Furiously, they even out all differences, in an obsessive and passionate kind of levelling. Whoever doesn't like them wants to kill them."[401]

The four types of antisemitism expression are interrelated in insidious ways. Each lays the groundwork for those that follow it in the typology. Each encourages and fortifies those that precede it in the list. In a country where you find organized public antisemitism, you will almost certainly find organized private antisemitism (it may even be legally required), violent antisemitism, and, almost certainly, rampant and escalating degradation antisemitism.

THE PURSUIT OF PEACE

Humankind cannot flourish without peace. We cannot do the things that really matter—look after each other, educate our children, be healthy, live creative lives, protect the environment, build beautiful buildings, die peacefully—if we are consumed and distracted by conflict. Of course, human beings will not agree on many fundamental issues—political issues, religious issues, cultural issues. They will not agree on them, nor should they just for the sake of agreement. The right kind of disagreement sparks discussion that enhances life and helps achieve truth and understanding, even when conflict is not resolved. Disagreement can even be enjoyable (not always).

What matters is how disagreement occurs. It must be done with integrity, respect, restraint, discipline, and with full recognition that on almost every issue there can be more than one reasonable point of view. This does not mean that disagreement cannot be rigorous and vigorous. It does mean that disagreement should happen in a way that does not disrupt peace. And, by the way, difference in identity does

401 Note 4, p. 120.

not inevitably lead to disagreement on issues. Different people—races, religions, interest groups, nations, states—can agree with each other on many important things.

Identity politics has damaged the way we disagree. It has disrupted peace. It has invaded every aspect of our discourse. It routinely repudiates the axiom that there is always some common ground. It eliminates opportunities for agreement. It drives us into our corners. Uncompromising insistence on individual identities repudiates universalist philosophical movements, including the concepts of a common humanity and universal human rights. It rejects the ideal that all citizens have equal rights as individuals, and that rights reside with individuals and not groups. It denies justice as fairness. It encourages conflict.

If we wish for peace, we must begin with a critical re-examination of identity politics. This will not be easy. It is too much to hope that a worldwide reversal of this powerful social movement will occur. It is too much to hope that we will peacefully and fully embrace the idea of a common humanity and move forward together. One important reason is that, in many cases, identity politics, despite the evils of its excesses, has ethical and historic justification which give it enormous traction and legitimacy. Who could deny, for example, the legitimacy of many of the grievances of women, persons of colour, indigenous peoples, and members of the LGBTQ community, across the world? They were never properly protected by any concept of common humanity. Quite the contrary. For so long, self-interest, privilege, and prejudice cleverly hid behind a vague and superficial idea of common humanity. Realization of this explains, in part, the tenacious grip of identity politics. But the realization and the justification do not justify a wholesale and undiscriminating acceptance of politics which stands in the way of peace.

Sometimes it seems as if there is no peace for the Jewish community in particular. Within the Jewish community, there is disagreement about so many things, even about who is a legitimate member of the community and about the importance of Judaism. As for the outside world, the Jewish community is pitted against hostile Muslim and Arab communities, suspicious Christian churches, and a worldwide

149

general antisemitism that is said to be on the rise. The rise of identity politics, fractious and unyielding, and the development of social media have contributed to this turmoil. Non-Jewish groups find it that much easier to be antagonistic and unyielding towards Jews. Jews themselves adopt many of the aggressive strategies of modern identity politics. They make the kind of complaints and claims that all committed identity groups make. They claim to be oppressed and marginalized. They see antisemitism everywhere, without having a clear concept of the different kinds of antisemitism and the implications of each. Their response to antisemitism is incoherent. They lash out. Thus, they damage their own interests and obstruct peace.

The modern Arab point of view is not hard to understand. It is largely attributable to the circumstances surrounding creation of the State of Israel, and to subsequent Israeli policies concerning Palestine and the Palestinians. Arab hostility towards Jews is, of course, fully reciprocated. The dispute between Jews and Arabs is primarily geo-political, mostly about territory and dispossession. It is not religious, theological, ethnic, or cultural in nature. This makes a solution to the dispute more possible. A solution will be difficult, but the pursuit of peace requires we search for one. There are roads to be travelled.

Often, careless, confusing, and inflammatory rhetoric stands in the way of understanding and peace between Arabs and Jews. Accusations—Zionist, anti-Zionist, antisemite—fly thick and fast. Many, and not just Arabs, claim that Zionism and Palestinian history exemplify continuing colonial oppression of an indigenous population. They call "Zionists" those they consider responsible for this perceived oppression. They themselves are known as "anti-Zionists." Some anti-Zionists, without considering the matter very carefully, regard all Jews as Zionists, although this is clearly not the case. For these anti-Zionists, to hate Zionists is to hate all Jews. Anti-Zionism becomes an all-encompassing antisemitism. But not all anti-Zionists believe that all Jews are Zionists. It is wrong for a Jew to label all anti-Zionists as antisemites. To do so is often a way of sidestepping and obscuring the genuine grievances that Arabs and others have against Israel; anyone who speaks out about those grievances must be antisemitic. None of this is helpful. The charge that anti-Zionism is antisemitism impedes progress towards resolving conflict. It suggests that any attempt to solve the Palestinian problem is driven by Jew-hatred.

The relationship between Jews and Christians is more parlous than the relationship between Jews and Arabs and more difficult to resolve. Deicide—the assertion that the Jews killed Christ—has been a core idea of the Christian church. To this day, supersessionism, sometimes called replacement theology, holds considerable theological sway in Christianity. Supersessionism is the idea that followers of Jesus replaced the Jews as the chosen people of God, and that Christianity, a newer covenant, is a far better religion than Judaism which was merely a prologue to Christianity. Some believe that these ideas laid the philosophical groundwork for much oppression of the Jews, including the Holocaust (see Chapter 4). There have been efforts within the Christian church to correct these mistakes, but they have been unconvincing.

CODA: THREE MINUTES IN POLAND

When I wrote about Jews as victims (Chapter 6), I told a few stories about individual Jews. Some things can only be truly understood by thinking about individuals. A description of what happened to large groups or wide communities doesn't tell the tale. That is one of the flaws of identity politics. At the end of the day, the tragedy of not having peace and justice is the tragedy of individuals. At the end of the day, all tragedy is individual.

In 1938, Glenn Kurtz's grandfather, David Kurtz, shot a home movie which included three minutes footage of the Jewish community in the Polish town of Nasielsk.[402] Nasielsk was David Kurtz's home town (he

---

402 See Glenn Kurtz, *Three Minutes in Poland: Discovering a Lost World in a 1938 Family Film* (New York: Farrar, Straus and Giroux, 2014). See also University of California Television, *Three Minutes in Poland: Discovering a Lost World in*

emigrated to the United States in the 1890s), and in 1938 he was on a European holiday which included a visit to the place of his birth. You can see the film on the website of the United States Holocaust Memorial Museum.[403] The Museum website describes what it depicts this way: "Street scenes, dark, people gathered, automobile. Interior shots of a restaurant (probably Owsianka) in a Jewish quarter in Nasielsk, Poland, many people looking inside the window in clear view. Several wonderful street scenes of people, especially children, in the Jewish quarter grinning and vying for the camera's attention. A sign above a shop indicates a grocery, 'Spozywczy.'"

Glenn Kurtz describes his grandfather's film more poetically: "[W]e see hundreds of faces with individual expressions. We see the patterns and colors of dresses, a sign over a doorway, flowers in a shop window. We see the intricacies of small-town society in the groups that form on the street. We see the way a hand gesture or the peculiar set of someone's mouth or brow defines a personality or a relationship . . . We see the prevalence of shoving as a means of communication."[404] I have watched this film many times. There is a cornucopia of individual and community life in its three minutes. The people it shows are full of energy and happiness, particularly the children. I am reminded of the pictures of French Jewish children, assembled by Serge Klarsfeld (see Chapter 6).

When David Kurtz made his film in the summer of 1938, Nasielsk had a population of about 4,500 people. Two-thirds of them were

a 1938 Family Film, in which Kurtz discusses his book. https://www.youtube.com/watch?v=d1_vYrs9kng (accessed January 8, 2022). See also Nina Siegal, "A Film Captures Jewish Life in a Polish Town Before the Nazis Arrived," *The New York Times* January 3, 2022 https://www.nytimes.com/2022/01/03/movies/three-minutes-a-lengthening-documentary.html?searchResultPosition=1 (accessed January 7, 2022). Siegal discussed Bianca Stigter's 2021 documentary about the footage called *Three Minutes—A Lengthening.*

403 https://collections.ushmm.org/search/catalog/irn1004329. See also https://www.ushmm.org/search/results.php?q=Nasielsk&q__src=&q__grp=&q__typ=&q__mty=Other&q__sty=&q__lng= for other Museum materials related to this story.

404 Kurtz, note 402, p.7.

Jewish. The Germans entered the town a year later, on September 4, 1939, just after they invaded Poland (Nasielsk was on the road to Warsaw). On December 3 they rounded up the Jewish population. Most were eventually sent to Treblinka where they were murdered.

The horror of what happened to the Jews of Nasielsk was described many years later by Maurice Chandler, then an old man living in Boca Raton, Florida.[405] In the Kurtz film, Maurice Chandler appears briefly as a thirteen-year-old called Moszek Tuchendler living in Nasielsk. When the Germans arrived, Moszek escaped across the Bug River to Bialystok. Later he became trapped in the Warsaw Ghetto with his parents and brother. His parents died. Moszek escaped from the Ghetto in May 1941, got work as farm hand, and with the help of friendly Poles changed his name (to Zdzislaw Plywacz) and identity (he pretended to be a Roman Catholic Polish orphan). He survived the war[406] and found his way to the United States where he became a scrap-metal dealer and changed his name once again.

Only about eighty of the 3,000 Jews living in Nasielsk in 1939 survived the war. Sixty settled in Israel.

---

405 See "Oral History Interview with Morris Tuchendler Chandler," United States Holocaust Memorial Museum, https://collections.ushmm.org/search/catalog/irn513756 (accessed January 7, 2021).

406 For a detailed account of Maurice's wartime experiences, see Kurtz, note 402, especially chapter 11.

ACKNOWLEDGEMENTS

Thanks in particular to: Philippe Poussier for his unstinting encourage-ment, and in particular for alerting me to important books by Stefan Zweig and Alain Finkielkraut; Murray Glow for his profusion of insights and steadfast support; the late Marie-Ange Garrigue for encouraging me when I needed encouragement; Heather Mitchell for her uncom-promising and helpful criticism of some parts of the book; Patty and Nicole Himel for talking to me about Marcel; Beverley Slopen, my agent, for representing my interests energetically, as always; and to my wife, Cynthia, for everything. Needless to say, all of these people may well disagree with some (perhaps most) of what I have to say.

ABOUT THE AUTHOR

Born in England and raised in Manitoba, Philip Slayton is a Canadian lawyer and writer. He is the best-selling author of *Lawyers Gone Bad: Money, Sex and Madness in Canada's Legal Profession*, and *Mighty Judgment: How the Supreme Court of Canada Runs Your Life*, among other books. A Rhodes Scholar, he has been a Woodrow Wilson Fellow and President of PEN Canada. Married to writer Cynthia Wine, he lives in Toronto and Nova Scotia.

INDEX

INDEX